# THE
# GRIEF RECOVERY
## HANDBOOK

# THE
# GRIEF RECOVERY
## HANDBOOK

### 20TH ANNIVERSARY EXPANDED EDITION

*THE ACTION PROGRAM FOR*

*MOVING BEYOND DEATH, DIVORCE,*

*AND OTHER LOSSES*

*INCLUDING HEALTH, CAREER, AND FAITH*

JOHN W. JAMES AND RUSSELL FRIEDMAN

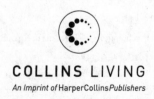

**COLLINS** LIVING

*An Imprint of* HarperCollins*Publishers*

HarperCollins books may be purchased for educational, business, or sales promotional use. For information please write: Special Markets Department, Harper-Collins Publishers, 10 East 53rd Street, New York, NY 10022.

*Designed by Elina D. Nudelman*

---

The Library of Congress had catalogued the revised edition ISBN as follows:

James, John W.
    The grief recovery handbook : the action program for moving beyond death, divorce, and other losses / John W. James and Russell
    Friedman.—Rev. ed.
        p.   cm.

    ISBN 0-06-220712-1

    1. Grief.   2. Loss (Psychology)   I. Friedman, Russell.
    II. Title.
    BF575.G7J36 1998
    152.8—dc21                                                                98-16555

---

ISBN 978-0-06-220712-8
12   13   14   15   16   WBC/RRD   10   9   8   7   6   5   4   3   2   1

*For the son I never knew.—J.W.J.*

*For my mom—you were my champion!—R.F.*

*And to all of you who are moving beyond loss.*

# Contents

## xii    Contents

# Introduction

It is unlikely that a person would wake up one morning and say, "Grief, what a concept, I think I'll make it my life's work." That is not how it happened for either of us. We are John W. James and Russell Friedman, and together we represent the Grief Recovery Institute.

Here is a little outline of our lives, the institute, and the evolution of *The Grief Recovery Handbook*.

John was thrust painfully into this arena by the death of a child in 1977. After discovering a successful process for completing his grief, he continued his career in the solar energy design business. Acquaintances who had heard of his loss and recovery experience brought their friends who were dealing with loss. Soon John was spending as much time with grievers as with contractors, and finding his work with the former more rewarding. After a while, he realized that grief recovery was what he was meant to do. As a direct result of John's awareness, the Grief Recovery Institute was established.

Russell's introduction to grief recovery came not as the

result of a death but in response to a second divorce coupled with a bankruptcy. He never would have equated his circumstances with the word *grief* had he not been dragged to a lecture on grief recovery presented by John. At that lecture Russell realized that there might be a solution for his overwhelmingly painful feelings. The following day, he showed up at the Grief Recovery Institute as a volunteer. Twenty-one years later, he is still there.

The Grief Recovery Institute has been guided by a primary principle, *to deliver grief recovery assistance to the largest number of people in the shortest period of time.* To meet this goal, the institute established Outreach Programs throughout the United States and Canada. Feedback from those fledgling support groups indicated a clear need for additional support. The first version of *The Grief Recovery Handbook* was written and self-published to meet that demand. The success of the book made it clear that a mainstream publisher might be able to extend our reach and help even more grievers.

In 1988 HarperCollins (then Harper & Row) agreed to publish an updated edition, ensuring that many more grievers would have access to effective help in overcoming loss. This has been a very successful collaboration. The nationwide wingspan of HarperCollins has helped *The Grief Recovery Handbook* become available in every community, large and small. With availability has come recovery.

There is no accurate way to determine how many people have been helped by the three previous editions of *The Grief Recovery Handbook.* Conservative estimates would indicate that the number is more than a million people. While we are excited and pleased to have the chance to update the handbook, we must begin by acknowledging and thanking all of you who were responsible for the success of the earlier ones.

We want to give special recognition to the thousands of grieving people who have shared their lives through their calls and letters. It is your feedback and input that have encouraged us to make the changes that in turn will help many more hurting people. We also want to acknowledge the thousands of professionals who have embraced our work. Your suggestions and encouragement have been invaluable.

In 1998, HarperCollins published *The Grief Recovery Handbook, Revised Edition*. In the ten years following the 1988 edition, we had made tremendous strides in helping grieving people. The revised edition allowed us to pass along to the readers the improved actions that lead to recovery. The new material in that edition supported John's original idea that, *"with correct information and correct choices, a person can recover from any significant loss."*

It is now 2008, and another ten years have passed. Working with thousands more grievers, we have learned more and better ways to help people deal with grief. We are thrilled to be able to pass along what we've learned to make recovery more accessible and more possible for you. The new material is contained in Part Four, which begins on page 167.

We have lectured and consulted for every imaginable type of organization—universities, medical schools, hospitals, alcohol and drug rehabilitation programs, funeral homes and cemeteries, public and private schools, as well as social, religious, and philosophical groups—throughout the world. While this list may be academically impressive, we would like you to disregard it. *Although the list is intellectually accurate, it is emotionally irrelevant.*

As our personal stories illustrate, we did not come to our careers in grief recovery by way of intellectual pursuit. We were jolted into this work by our broken hearts. Every one of you arrives at this book because your heart has been broken too. While you already know your heart is broken, your question might be, "What do I do about it?" This book has the answer. The concepts of grief recovery presented here represent a breakthrough in helping grieving people deal successfully with loss.

Most professionals have addressed grief from a conceptual, intellectual perspective. *This has often left grievers with much understanding—but very little recovery.* This book is focused totally on recovery from the emotional pain caused by death, divorce, and other losses.

For all of you struggling with unresolved grief issues, we know that the actions outlined in this book will lead you to completion of the pain caused by loss. We also know that recovery is not an easy journey. We know that your losses may have closed your heart down. If we could, we would be with you as you take the actions that will lead your heart to open again. You may be afraid to start, or you may get scared along the way. Please remember that hundreds of thousands of people have used these same actions. We know that they join us in encouraging you to move through your apprehension and begin the process of recovery.

We wish you good luck on your journey, and remain,
Of service,

*John & Russell*

# PART ONE

# *Seeing the Problem*

*If you are reading this book, there is a high probability that your heart is broken.*

It may have been caused by a death, either recent or long ago.

It may have been caused by a divorce or the breakup of a romantic relationship.

It may have been caused by any of the more than forty other losses that a person can encounter during a lifetime.

It could be caused by an awareness that your life is not as happy or fulfilling as you want it to be.

Regardless of the cause of your broken heart, you know how you feel, and it probably isn't good.

We are not going to tell you how you feel. You already know. And we will not tell you, "We know how you feel," because we don't. *Neither does anyone else.* At best, we remember how we felt when our losses occurred.

**Even though you've endured painful changes in the circumstances of your life, we are going to tell you what actions you need to take to regain a sense of well-being.**

## HOW TO USE *THE GRIEF RECOVERY HANDBOOK*

Don't jump ahead in your reading of this handbook. There is a difference between those who resolve their pain and those who don't. The ones who recover follow a well-defined plan. We want you to follow such a plan so that you can be successful.

This handbook is designed to give you the information necessary to recover from loss. It has much to offer anyone who truly wants to feel better. It will allow you to choose *completion* and *recovery* rather than *isolation* and *avoidance*. If you use it, one word at a time, it will accelerate your recovery tenfold.

Throughout the text are suggestions, notes, and guidelines. Please don't take any shortcuts. They can lead you unwittingly right back to old ideas that still won't work. Stay on track with this program and with your recovery.

### WARNING

This book is not intended as a teaching manual, so we alert you to avoid the temptation of thinking that reading this book or taking the actions in it prepares you to help others. We offer very specific Grief♥Recovery® Certification Programs for that purpose. At the back of the book are addresses and phone numbers to use in contacting us for more information about all of our programs.

# 1

# *Grief: A Neglected and Misunderstood Process*

Grief is the normal and natural reaction to loss of any kind. Therefore, the feelings you are having are also normal and natural for you. The problem is that we have all been socialized to believe that these feelings are abnormal and unnatural.

While grief is normal and natural, and clearly the most powerful of all emotions, it is also *the most neglected and misunderstood experience, often by both the grievers and those around them.*

*Grief is the conflicting feelings caused by the end of or change in a familiar pattern of behavior.* What do we mean by *conflicting feelings*? Let us explain by example. When someone you love dies after suffering a long illness, you may feel a sense of relief that your loved one's suffering is over. That is a positive feeling, even though it is associated with a death. At the same time, you may realize that you can no longer see or touch that person. This may be very painful for you. These conflicting feelings, relief and pain, are totally normal in response to death.

*What about divorce? Are there conflicting feelings too?* Yes. You may feel a genuine sense of freedom now that the battles are over. That is a positive feeling. At the same time, you may be afraid that you will never "find someone as beautiful/as good a provider." These conflicting feelings, freedom and fear, are also natural responses to loss.

All relationships have aspects of familiarity whether they are romantic, social, familial, or business. What other losses cause similar conflicting feelings? While death and divorce are obvious, many other loss experiences have been identified that can produce grief. Among them are:

> Death of a pet
> Moving
> Starting school
> Death of a former spouse
> Marriage
> Graduation
> End of addictions
> Major health changes
> Retirement
> Financial changes—positive or negative
> Holidays
> Legal problems
> Empty nest

Often these common life experiences are not seen as grieving events. We grieve for the loss of all relationships we deem significant—which are thus also emotional.

**If the major loss events in your life have not been associated with death, do not put this book down.**

After thirty years of working with grievers, we have identified several other losses, including loss of trust, loss of safety, and loss of control of one's body (physical or sexual abuse). Society still does not recognize these losses as grief issues.

Loss-of-trust events are experienced by almost everyone and can have a major, lifelong negative impact. You may have experienced a loss of trust in a parent, a loss of trust in God, or a loss of trust in any other relationship. Is loss of trust a grief issue? The answer is *yes*. And the problem of dealing with the grief it causes remains the same. Grief is normal and natural, but we have been ill prepared to deal with it. *Grief is about a broken heart, not a broken brain.* All efforts to heal the heart with the head fail because the head is the wrong tool for the job. It's like trying to paint with a hammer—it only makes a mess.

Almost all intellectual comments are preceded by the phrase, "Don't feel bad." In 1977, when John's infant son died, a well-meaning friend said, "Don't feel bad—you can have other children." The intellectually accurate statement that John had the physical capability to have other children was not only irrelevant, it was unintentionally abusive, because it belittled his natural and normal emotions. John felt bad, his heart was broken.

When Russell and his first wife divorced, he was devastated. A friend said, "Don't feel bad—you'll do better next time." Most of the comments that grievers hear following a loss, while intellectually accurate, are emotionally barren. As a direct result of these conflicting ideas, a griever often feels confused and frustrated, feelings that lead to emotional isolation.

Since most of us have been socialized to attempt to resolve all issues with our intellect, grief remains a huge problem.

This intellectual focus has even led to academic articles that suggest gender is an issue in grief. We recognize that males and females are socialized differently, but our experience indicates that males and females are similarly limited when it comes to dealing with sad, painful, and negative feelings. Feelings themselves are without gender. There is no such thing as girl sad or boy sad, girl happy or boy happy.

We are not saying that intellect is totally useless in regard to grief. In fairness, you are reading a book, which is an intellectual activity. The book will ask you to understand concepts and to take actions, so clearly there is a degree of intellect involved.

## GRIEF AND RECOVERY

For many, seeing this book's title is the first time they have ever seen the terms "grief" and "recovery" used together. Religious and spiritual leaders have pointed out for centuries that we should look at loss as an opportunity for personal spiritual development. Yet in modern life, moving through intense emotional pain has become such a misunderstood process that most of us have very little idea of how to respond to loss.

What do we mean by recovery? Recovery means feeling better. Recovery means claiming your circumstances instead of your circumstances claiming you and your happiness. Recovery is finding new meaning for living, without the fear of being hurt again. Recovery is being able to enjoy fond memories without having them precipitate painful feelings of regret or remorse. Recovery is acknowledging that it is perfectly all right to feel sad from time to time and to talk about those feelings no matter how those around you react. Recovery is being able to forgive others when they say or do things that you know are based on their lack of knowledge about grief. Recovery is one day realizing that your ability to talk about the loss you've experienced is indeed normal and healthy.

Most important, recovery means acquiring the skills that we should have been taught in childhood. These skills allow us to deal with loss directly. Most of us are aware that there is no guarantee that our loved ones will be alive when we get home. Those who have experienced divorce also realize there is no guarantee that our spouse will love us when we get home. The skills of grief recovery will heal your heart if it gets broken and in turn allow you to participate 100 percent in all of your relationships. With the knowledge and freedom brought about by completing losses comes the additional benefit of allowing ourselves to love as totally as possible.

Obviously, recovering from a significant emotional loss is not an easy task. Taking the actions that lead to recovery will require your attention, open-mindedness, willingness, and courage.

## STAYING OPEN TO GRIEF

We've all heard the statement, "The only things certain in life are death and taxes." Those of you who are reading this book know that one more item must be added to these certainties: loss. We all experience loss many times in our lives. Despite the universality of the experience of loss, people know very little about recovery from it.

What we do know about grievers is that they've always

wanted to recover. They seek help from all available sources. Grievers attend support groups, read pamphlets, buy books. After having done all these things, they're still confronted with the fact that our entire society is ill equipped to help them bring the grieving experience to a successful conclusion. Over time the pain of unresolved grief is cumulative. Whether caused by a death, divorce, or other type of loss, incomplete recovery can have a lifelong negative impact on a person's capacity for happiness.

## GRIEF RECOVERY: HOW DOES IT WORK?

**Recovery from loss is achieved by a series of small and correct choices made by the griever.**

Sadly, most of us have not been given the necessary information with which to make correct choices. This book takes on the specific challenge of reeducating anyone who has a genuine desire to discover and complete the emotional pain caused by loss. We know that the principles discussed here work. They work for those who have experienced the death of a loved one, a divorce, or any other loss.

The death of a loved one produces emotions that can be described as *the feeling of reaching out for someone who has always been there, only to find that when we need them one more time, they are no longer there.*

Some of you will be reading this book for help in dealing

with a problematic relationship with someone who has died. We might call this a relationship with a "less than loved one." For you, the feeling is one of *reaching out for someone who has never been there for you, and still isn't.* This is also true for those of you who need to discover and complete the unfinished emotions attached to a living person with whom you have a less than fulfilling relationship.

It is almost always true that loss as a result of divorce falls into the "less than loved one" category. Although divorce severs the marital, sexual, and social ties, *divorce does not complete emotional ties.* Without successful recovery, it is common for divorcés—male and female—to repeat their mistakes in ensuing relationships.

## AN INCOMPLETE PAST MAY DOOM THE FUTURE

We have no moral, legal, religious, or social position about divorce. We have a very simple belief that everyone involved in a divorce is a griever. That includes children, parents, siblings, and friends of the couple. This attitude makes it easy for us. We always know that the primary issue is unresolved grief.

Divorce (or a broken romantic relationship) produces grief. This can become a life-limiting reality that negatively affects future relationships. Incomplete grief over a former spouse will dictate fearful choices. Incomplete grief will create hypervigilant self-protection from further emotional pain. Sadly, this excess of caution limits the ability to be

open, trusting, and loving, dooming the next relationship to failure.

We hope you will recognize the need to go back and
complete prior relationships in order to enhance the possibility of success in your current one. For those of you
 still feeling isolated and alone, we hope this book gives
you the courage to complete prior relationships so you
can venture forth into the world and seek a new, healthy
romantic relationship.

# 2

# Compounding the Problem

Grief is difficult enough without added complications. Unfortunately, many factors can compound our reactions to loss and limit our recovery. This chapter will alert you to some of the pitfalls that can stall or short-circuit your recovery.

## CONFUSION ABOUT STAGES

Many people are familiar with the pioneering work of Dr. Elisabeth Kubler-Ross, who identified five emotional stages that a dying person may go through after being diagnosed with a terminal illness. She identified those stages as denial, anger, bargaining, depression, and acceptance.

One result of Dr. Kubler-Ross's work is that many people now tend to apply the concept of stages to other aspects of human emotion. Grief, which follows death, divorce, and other losses, should not, however, be regarded in terms of stages. The nature and intensity of feelings caused by a loss

relate to the individuality and uniqueness of the relationship.

While Dr. Kubler-Ross's contributions brought heightened
awareness about the process of *dying,* her work has been accompanied by some unfortunate collateral damage. Many people,
professionals and the general public alike, have attempted to apply her stages to the emotions that arise after a loss. She identified denial as the first stage that follows notification of a terminal
illness. Absent other helpful information, her work has often
been misinterpreted to imply that denial is also a stage that a
person experiences following a death or divorce.

In all our years working with grievers, we have yet to be ap-
proached by someone who is in "denial" that a loss had occurred.
The very first thing they say to us is, "My mother died," or, "My
dog died," or, "My wife divorced me." These statements reflect
absolutely no denial that a loss has occurred. If you are reading
this book, *you are not in denial* that you have experienced a loss.

## WHAT ABOUT ANGER?

Much of the literature about grief contends that anger is always a factor in loss. Respectfully, we disagree. Anger is sometimes associated with the circumstances of a loss. It is often a
factor in our difficult relationships with less than loved ones.
Yet the presumption of anger is both incorrect and dangerous.
A death often involves no anger at all. One brief account illustrates the point.

"My ninety-two-year-old grandmother, with whom I had a
wonderful relationship, became ill and died. Blessedly, it happened quickly, so she did not suffer very much. I am pleased

about that. I had just spent time with her and told her how much I cared about her. I am very happy about that. There was a funeral ceremony that accurately portrayed her. Many people came and talked about her. I loved that. At the funeral, a helpful friend reminded me to say good-bye. I did and am glad. I am not angry."

This is a true story. If the story had been different, it would have created different feelings. If the grandson had not been able to talk to his grandmother before she died, he might have been angry at the circumstances that prevented him from doing so. If she had been a less than loved one, he might have been angry that she died before he had a chance to repair the relationship.

Please do not believe that anger is an automatic part of unresolved grief. Some grievers will be angry, and others won't. But if anger is there, we will find it and complete it.

## COMMON RESPONSES

While there are no stages of grief, many grievers do experience some very common responses.

*Reduced concentration.* A griever is in the bedroom. He has an idea about getting something from the kitchen. Upon arrival in the kitchen, he has no earthly idea why he is there or what he went there to get. A preoccupation with the emotions of loss and an inability to concentrate seem to be universal responses to grief.

*A sense of numbness.* Grievers typically report to us that the first reaction they experience after notification of a loss is a sense of numbness. This numbness can be physical, emotional, or both. The numbness lasts a different length of time for each person. Rarely have we seen this sense of numbness last more than several hours. This reaction is often mislabeled as denial.

*Disrupted sleep patterns.* Grievers report either not being able to sleep or sleeping too much—or both, alternately.

*Changed eating habits.* Grievers tell us that they have no appetite or that they eat nonstop—or both, alternately.

*Roller coaster of emotional energy.* Grievers talk about going up and down and in and out of feelings. As a direct result of these emotional highs and lows, grievers often feel emotionally and physically drained. This reaction will be discussed in depth later in the book.

These are all normal and natural responses to loss. Their duration is unique to every individual. We will not predict for you how long they should last. They do not always occur. They are not stages.

*There are no stages of grief.* But people will always try to fit themselves into a defined category if one is offered to them. Sadly, this is particularly true if the offer comes from a powerful authority such as a therapist, clergyperson, or doctor.

*Do not allow anyone to create any time frames or stages for you.*

**There are no absolutes in grief. There are no reactions so universal that all, or even most, people will experience**

**them. There is only one unalterable truth: All relation-
ships are unique.**

## GETTING OVER OR GETTING COMPLETE

One of the most damaging pieces of misinformation is the
idea that you can "never get over" the death of a child. This
absolutely incorrect claim is made to parents whose child has
died, but it is also made in connection with other losses. Grieving parents and others then seek out information and emotions
to match the untruth.

It is more accurate to ask, "Is it possible to forget your child
or, for that matter, your spouse or parent?" Clearly the answer
is no! "Not forgetting" becomes incorrectly entangled with the
idea of "not getting over." This crippling idea keeps the griever's
heart eternally broken, does not allow for recovery of any kind,
and, more often than not, severely limits any fond memories
associated with the relationship.

Last January we were talking with a woman whose daughter had committed suicide in the month of February several
years earlier. As we talked, she told us that as February ap-
proached, she thought about her daughter more and more.
Many of her thoughts and feelings were painful. We acknowledged the truth of her feelings and the logic of the renewed
intensity as the painful anniversary date neared. Her eyes
welled up with tears as she talked about her relationship with
her daughter. She said, "My heart is permanently broken."

Most people would accept her comment and move on. But

we didn't. Instead, we asked her whether she often had fond memories of her daughter. She said yes. We asked how she felt when those fond and pleasant memories came to mind. She said they felt good. So we asked, "When you are having pleasant memories, does your heart feel broken?" "No," she said, "it doesn't."

We then suggested that she not use the phrase "permanently broken heart" to describe herself. We recommended that she say instead, "Sometimes when I am reminded of her struggles and her death, my heart feels broken. Other times, remembering her wonderful qualities, I feel happy and pleased to share my memories about her."

There is a common and false picture created by grievers, by professionals, and by the literature: "Because I haven't forgotten her and still sometimes have feelings about her, I am not over the pain of the loss." This tragic setup is guaranteed to restrict and deflate the life of the griever.

## WHEN IS IT TIME TO BEGIN TO RECOVER?

Earlier we mentioned that a sense of numbness and a reduced ability to concentrate are typical for grievers. In spite of those responses, grievers are willing to *talk about the circumstances of the loss* and to *review the relationship they had*. (This review occurs with all losses.) Consequently, effective grief recovery can begin almost immediately. It is very easy to tap into that review and discover a multitude of undelivered emotional communications. Even the most loving and complete of relationships will end with some incompleteness.

The accuracy of our memories is heightened by the loss itself. This can be an ideal opportunity to harvest an incredible collection of memories. Grievers need and want to talk about their losses. It is typical for a family to talk immediately afterwards about the family member who died. It is equally common following a divorce, retirement, pet loss, job loss, or physical change to talk about the good and bad experiences within those relationships or events.

Talking about loss and about relationships is wonderful and good, but it is generally not enough to allow us to feel complete. We need to take additional actions to help complete the pain we discover as we talk about our relationships.

One of our saddest experiences involves people who have signed up to participate in a Grief Recovery Seminar or a Grief Recovery Outreach Program but don't appear at the session. Occasionally, they call to cancel saying, "My therapist said I'm not ready to do my grief work yet."

Here is a little two-part quiz that graphically answers the question, "When do I begin to recover?"

1. If you fell down and gashed your leg and blood was pouring out, would you immediately seek medical attention? The obvious answer is yes.
2. If circumstances and events conspired to break your heart, would you seek attention immediately, or would you allow yourself to bleed to death emotionally? Pick one!

Is it ever too soon to begin to recover? *No.* The first ten years of our grief recovery careers were devoted to helping funeral directors, cemeterians, and clergy better assist grieving people. Clearly, those professionals are helping grievers in the hours and days immediately following a death. *It is never too soon to address your grief.*

## SUICIDE, MURDER, AIDS, AND OTHER
## TRAGIC CIRCUMSTANCES

Emotional isolation is a major problem for grievers. Focusing on the cause of a loss, such as suicide, murder, AIDS, or another tragic circumstance, tends to increase this isolation.

Grief is by definition emotional. That is not to say that the cause of death does not generate emotion. Clearly, if someone we love dies in tragic circumstances, we will have volumes of feeling about the unfairness of it all. After acknowledging that we have been affected by the circumstances of a death, we must move immediately toward two larger truths.

The first is a painful question. Would you miss your loved one any less if he or she had died some other way? The answer is always *no*.

And second, what is left emotionally unfinished for you as the result of this death?

Earlier we talked about *anger* and *denial* not being helpful words for grievers. *Closure* is another unhelpful and inaccurate word. Following jury verdicts, the media rush in, thrusting cameras and microphones in grievers' faces. They ask whether the decision has brought "closure." The answer is always *no*.

Lawsuits may or may not serve justice. When the suit is over, however, you are still left with what is emotionally unfinished between yourself and your loved one who has died. At best, the lawsuit completes the crime or the infraction. A lawsuit cannot help you become *emotionally complete*.

We have seen people make a life cause out of the circumstances that took their loved one. We find nothing wrong with that. All of us in society benefit from heightened awareness and increased oversight regarding the law, medicine, and other issues. Our lives are enhanced by the tireless efforts of these reformers. Sadly, though, most of them remain incomplete with their loved one who died. Their tremendous expenditure of energy keeps them constantly distracted from the primary issue, their own unresolved grief.

Some of you will have cause to pursue lawsuits, either civil or criminal, relating to the death or mistreatment of a loved one. We encourage you to do the actions of grief recovery first. Completion will make you a better advocate. You will have more energy. Most important, you will not operate under the illusion that a lawsuit or judgment will heal your broken heart.

## THE "G" WORD

An often misused word applied to grief is *guilt*. At the Grief Recovery Institute, we call it the "G" word. We almost never introduce that word to grievers, because it is rarely the right word.

A standard painful interaction at the Grief Recovery Institute sounds like this:

GRIEVER: My son committed suicide. I feel so guilty.
INSTITUTE: Did you ever do anything with intent to harm your son?
GRIEVER: No. (*This is an almost universal response.*)
INSTITUTE: The dictionary definition of guilt implies intent to harm. Since you had no intent to harm, can you put the "G" word back in the dictionary? You are probably devastated enough by the death of your son, you don't need

to add to it by hurting yourself with an incorrect word that distorts your feelings.

GRIEVER: Really? I never thought of it that way.

INSTITUTE: Are there some things that you wish had ended *different, better, or more?*

GRIEVER: Oh, yes.

And then the floodgates open.

In rare instances, people have done things with intent to harm. When that is true, an apology helps to remove any obstacles to completion.

## *SURVIVOR*: ANOTHER INACCURATE WORD

You may have noticed that throughout this book, you have not seen the word *survivor*. This is intentional. *Survivor* is intellectually accurate. It implies that the griever has outlived someone else. But we have discovered that the word *survivor* tends to act as both a definition and a diagnosis and often keeps people stuck in a dangerous and painful rut. For example, you don't survive someone else's suicide. You may survive if someone tries to murder you, but not when they attempt or commit suicide.

More important, the word *survivor* defines the griever and causes him or her to constantly revisit the circumstances about the loss. Being a survivor often becomes an identity. The strong, habituated identification with pain can become who the griever is. It is not uncommon for grievers to get more caught up in defining themselves and their pain than in completing the unfinished emotional aspects of the relationship. All the while, they are liable to remain incomplete with the person who died.

We know there are groups organized around and limited to those who have experienced specific losses, such as suicide, murder, AIDS, death of a child, and even divorce. Since we believe that grievers are already isolated in our society, we also believe that segregating grievers by *type of loss* adds to that isolation. However, we recognize that meeting together with others who have had a similar experience is not without its comforts.

Our beliefs, confirmed by twenty years of hands-on experience, are that:

> All relationships are unique; therefore all recovery is individual.
>
> Focusing on the shared intellectual truth (type of loss) does nothing to promote the process of recovery.
>
> Isolation by type of loss may have short-term value but does not encourage long-term solutions.

## THERE IS NOTHING WRONG WITH YOU

Major losses resulting from death, divorce, and other causes are usually not common occurrences. Therefore, we are generally not familiar with the thoughts and feelings we experience following losses. It is inevitable that we fall back on whatever information we have learned in the past to try to deal with our responses to the conflicting feelings caused by a loss event. Throughout this book, we refer to the fact that most of us were socialized incorrectly on the topic of grief. However, nothing we say here is intended in any way to condemn society, anyone's parents, or any institutions. We do not believe that one generation intentionally hands down misinformation to the next. We believe that people teach what they know, which is most likely what they were taught.

If you have found that the available information and support have not been adequate in helping you recover from loss, it is not because of what's wrong with you—it's because there is a lack of correct information. If you're reading this book, it means you're open to your grief. It means you're open to beginning a process of recovery that will enhance your life rather than limit it. If you're reading this book, it's because of what's right with you, not what's wrong.

# 3

# We Are Ill Prepared to Deal with Loss

Shortly after the loss you experienced, you probably became acutely aware of how ill prepared you were to deal with the conflicting mass of emotions we call grief. The same is true for almost everyone in our society. We are far better prepared to deal with minor accidents than we are to deal with grief. We receive more education about simple first aid than we do about death, divorce, and other emotional losses.

Stop and consider your own experience. In grade school, you took a class on first aid; in high school, you took a class on health and safety. The local Red Cross offers classes on first aid in the community. Nationwide we have a convenient 911 number to call in case of emergency. At some level, we're all prepared to take action if an accident occurs in our presence. How many classes have you taken on how to deal with the grief caused by significant emotional loss?

We think it's strange that we all know what to do if someone breaks an arm, but very few people are prepared to assist grievers. Eight million people become new grievers each year owing to death alone. In addition, the divorce rate exceeds 45 percent. This statistic does not include relationships that were never formalized by marriage. Many millions of relationships end annually, affecting not only the couple but children, parents, other relatives, and friends. It is estimated that more than fourteen million pets die per year in the United States alone. When you add the many millions of loss experiences related to retirement, job loss or change, medical problems, and major financial changes, the numbers are staggering.

## WE'RE TAUGHT HOW TO ACQUIRE THINGS, NOT WHAT TO DO WHEN WE LOSE THEM

In our formative years, an overwhelming emphasis is placed on learning how to acquire things in order to make life successful and happy.

In early childhood, we try to acquire our parents' praise. Later we try to acquire toys at Christmas or Hanukkah by being good. We try to earn high grades in school in order to gain approval. We try to look attractive to our peers so we'll be accepted. This process of learning how to acquire objects and attention continues into our adult lives. Certainly the advertising industry understands this phenomenon: marketing campaigns focus on finding happiness and contentment through the acquisition of things.

While we have learned much about acquiring things, we have precious little accurate information on what to do when we lose them.

Loss is inevitable. Sometimes loss is even predictable. In spite of these truths, we receive no formal training in how to respond to events that are guaranteed to happen and sure to cause pain and disruption. We are even advised not to learn about dealing with loss—or at the very least, not to talk about it. "What's done is done." "You have to move on." "Don't burden others with your feelings." The list goes on and on.

We are all liable to face several major losses in our lives. We must acknowledge that much of what we've learned about processing the feelings caused by loss is incorrect. In fact, if we had no knowledge about dealing with grief, we would be better off than we are operating with what we currently know. Most of us rely on old ideas to deal with whatever crisis confronts us. Even though we could show you that most of the ideas you learned about dealing with grief are not helpful, you may fall back on them when faced with the painful thoughts and feelings caused by loss. We typically do the same actions the same way, over and over. All actions, physical and emotional, become habitual. This is actually good news, being able to develop and maintain habits. The crucial step is to develop some helpful habits for dealing with grief.

First, in order to develop a new habit, you must become aware of the need to have a new habit. If you are reading this book, you are probably already aware that you need more effective information and habits for dealing with grief. Second, you must learn the component parts or skills necessary to build the habit. In the case of grief, this means identifying the ideas that do not work and replacing them with ideas that do. Third, you must practice the new ideas so that you can turn them into habits.

As you work your way through this book, you will be learning new ideas and practicing them. This is essential to the goal of completing the pain caused by loss. After working through this book, you will have much better habits for dealing with any losses or disappointments that occur in your life.

## WE'RE TAUGHT MYTHS ABOUT DEALING WITH GRIEF

Before we can discuss what recovery is, it's important to look at what it isn't. We must be clear about why we need to find a new way to deal with loss. We begin by clarifying our understanding of how we have dealt with loss in the past. We will use John's and Russell's experiences with loss as illustrations.

John's first memory about learning to deal with loss comes from when he was five years old:

> We had a family dog. This dog adopted me from the moment I arrived home from the hospital. When I was old enough to crawl, I'd pull the dog's tail and she'd let me get away with it. The dog would go everywhere with me. As I grew older, I tried to teach the dog to retrieve. (To this day, I'm not sure who taught whom to retrieve.) The dog always found a way to sleep with me each night. This drove my mother to distraction. But the dog and I were persistent and eventually Mom gave up. Then, one morning, I called to my dog and she wouldn't get up. I remember how cold she felt when I touched her. I remember being afraid. I called to my mother to help me. My mother told me that my dog had died. I'm certain she tried to explain what death was. I'm also certain she didn't know how.

For the next several days after the dog died, John cried a lot and spent a great deal of time in his room. "My parents felt inadequate in knowing what to do to help me," he remembers. Finally, in total frustration, John's father said:

> Don't cry—on Saturday we'll get you a new dog.

Now, that doesn't sound like such a profound sentence. But let's take a closer look. We learn by many different methods. One of these is called *influence learning.* A child is born into a family. During the first few years, the child's primary contact is with his or her parents. The child learns from watching and emulating what he sees his parents do. Usually, by eighteen to twenty-four months, the child has gained verbal skills. From this point forward, the child can not only see what his parents are doing but can understand what they say. John's father's words carried the following message:

> *Don't cry . . .*
> **Meaning: Don't feel bad.**
>
> *. . . on Saturday we'll get you a new dog.*
> **Meaning: Replace the loss.**

John believed his father. He began to form a belief about dealing with loss. He tried to follow his father's advice and not feel bad. To a young child who wanted his father's approval, this was a powerful communication from the most important authority figure in his life. As John explains, "I thought that if this is the way my father deals with death, then this is the way I'm supposed to deal with it."

Sure enough, on Saturday John's dad took him to the kennel and they got a new dog:

> *I still missed my old dog, but I didn't tell anyone. I didn't think they'd approve. After a long period of time, I actually forgot about my old dog. I also found it hard to love the new dog in the same way I'd loved my old dog, and I didn't know why.*

It's possible, in fact likely, that John couldn't love the new dog because he wasn't emotionally complete with the old dog.

When John was fourteen, he fell in love for the first time. It may have been puppy love, but it sure felt like the real thing to him.

> *It was wonderful. I was preoccupied with thoughts of her all the time. I had trouble eating and sleeping. The birds sang. I listened to love songs on the radio. I didn't hang out with my friends as much.*
>
> *When we broke up, I was devastated. This was a major loss for me. For days I wandered around like a wounded duck. Finally, my mother couldn't take it anymore.*

What his mother said was:

> *Don't feel bad—there are plenty of fish in the sea.*

By this point, John had gotten a clear idea about what to do when you lose something. He was going forth into life armed with two pieces of information on dealing with loss:

1. Don't feel bad.
2. Replace the loss.

Russell's childhood experiences were very similar to John's. "Don't feel bad" and "replace the loss" were used in the same kinds of circumstances.

Russell was unable to "not feel bad" when he felt bad. Loss experiences of all kinds made him feel sad. His sadness and tears were often met with comments like, "If you're going to cry, go to your room."

Russell struggled with hiding his feelings. He tried to talk with his mother about still feeling sad. She said to him, "Laugh and the whole world laughs with you, cry and you cry alone." It is heartbreaking to realize that when you are sad and might really benefit from some emotional understanding, you are taught to "be by yourself."

**Meaning: Grieve alone.**

It would be sad enough if it ended with feeling dismissed and misunderstood as a child. Unfortunately, though, this kind of misinformation becomes the foundation of lifelong habits, many of which directly interfere with our ability to be happy. Russell can remember too many times in his marriages when he stormed out of the house following an argument with his wife and drove aimlessly around the neighborhood. His car became a metaphor for his room as a child. The unchanging habit was to "grieve alone."

Since most of us are socialized in much the way John and Russell were, we usually think that it is correct for us to "isolate" or "grieve alone." Also tragic is the conclusion that stems from what we were taught. If I need to "grieve alone," then you do too. Thus, when a friend has experienced a loss, we often say, "Give her some space," or, "He needs to be alone."

John's experience following the death of his grandfather further illustrates the depth of society's belief in grieving alone.

*In 1958 my grandfather died. He was very important in my life. He was probably closer to me than my father was at that point. Every summer was spent at his farm. He taught me how to fish, hunt, and was the first to teach me how to play baseball.*

*When I was told he'd died, I was sitting in one of my high school classes. I can remember going numb. It was like being in a trance. After several minutes, I began to cry, and I suppose that made everyone uncomfortable. So they sent me to the principal's office so I could be by myself.*

Since they didn't know what to do, they sent John to the office to be alone.

*Once again, I assumed the adults around me knew what they were doing. This attitude of handling pain alone was further reinforced when I got home that night. My mother was sitting in the living room with her head down and was obviously crying. As soon as I saw her, I wanted to go to her so we could cry together. Both my father and my uncle came and said to me:*

*"Don't disturb your mother. She'll be okay in a little while."*

John and Russell now had three pieces of data on how to deal with loss.

1. Don't feel bad.
2. Replace the loss.
3. Grieve alone.

Not a single one of these lessons was going to be of any help to either of them.

While John was struggling with the death of his grandfather in Illinois, Russell was having a very difficult time as a teenager in Florida.

With each successive loss experience, Russell was constantly met with the same unhelpful ideas. Since he could not find a way to feel better using the ideas he had been taught, his life began to feel smaller and sadder. Each time a painful event occurred, he tried to "not feel bad" and to "grieve alone." He found himself believing that he would never be happy.

Finally, in desperation, he went to his mother. He told her that he could not seem to deal effectively with the thoughts and feelings that were troubling him. She looked at him sweetly and said, "Time heals all wounds."

**Meaning: Just give it time.**

Russell has absolutely no doubt that his mother loved him. She had no intent to harm her son. She merely passed on to him what had been taught to her.

In 1972 Russell and his first wife, Vivienne, divorced. Russell was devastated. He walked around like a zombie. Normally talkative and outgoing, he hardly spoke at all. Although he was not supposed to "feel bad," he was crushed. He felt awful. Having been taught to grieve alone, he found himself isolated a lot.

The early training to "replace the loss" was reinforced by well-meaning friends who suggested that he start dating. He didn't feel good, so the idea of dating didn't make sense to him. At the same time, he was being reminded that "time would heal him." The two ideas didn't go together. If replacing the loss was going to fix him, then he didn't have to wait for time to heal him. On the other hand, if time were to heal him, then maybe he shouldn't be in such a hurry to replace the loss.

The concept that time heals is probably responsible for more heartache than any other single wrong idea in our society. The terrible part is, it isn't true. It's one of those falsehoods that's been passed down from generation to generation.

The mistaken idea that after enough time passes something will magically change to make us whole again is preposterous. If we were dealing with any other human pain, no one would say, "Just give it time."

If you came across a person with a broken arm, you wouldn't say, "Just give it time." Just as broken bones should be properly set to heal and ultimately function again, so must the *emotional heart*.

We all know too many people whose hearts remain broken partly because they are waiting for time to heal them. Sadly, they come to believe it's true. People wait around for years with the idea that after a long enough period of time they will feel better again. Some of you reading this book already know this isn't true.

In one seminar, we asked people to raise their hands if they were still experiencing pain caused by a death or divorce that occurred more than twenty years ago. As expected, many people indicated this was true for them. They all believed that time would take care of the pain. We asked one woman whether twenty years didn't seem like too long a time to be waiting for recovery. She answered with a clear and classic statement: "Yes, it does, but I don't know what else to do." Can you imagine the pain and frustration? The years of waiting for some relief?

To illustrate the absurdity of waiting for time to heal, we ask this question. If you discovered that your car had a flat tire, would you pull up a chair next to the car and sit and wait for air to somehow get back into the tire? Seems silly, doesn't it?

Time itself does not heal; it is what you *do* within time that will help you complete the pain caused by loss.

Let's recap what John and Russell had learned about grief.

1. Don't feel bad.
2. Replace the loss.
3. Grieve alone.
4. Just give it time.

In 1957 Russell's grandmother died. She had been living with his family since Russell's mom went back to work. Grandma was the primary caretaker for Russell's younger brother, who is ten years younger than Russell. Russell had never felt particularly close to his grandmother. Sometimes he felt that she was mean to him. In those days in his family, it was not okay to talk negatively about family members—"blood is thicker than water" being the prevailing theme.

When his grandmother died, Russell recalls a family meeting. He remembers being told, "We have to be strong for your brother."

**Meaning: Be strong for others.**

There were no specific instructions on how to do that. "Be strong for others" is one of those expressions that sounds good but has no real value. Many years later, when Russell and his first wife divorced, his brain came up with, "Be strong for others." This was one of the few ideas Russell had for dealing with grief. In a heartbeat, he realized that this had no application to his divorce and he didn't have a clue what to do because he was the other.

In our twenty-plus years of helping grievers, "be strong" or "be strong for others" makes the top ten list as one of the most confusing of all ideas relating to loss. It is confusing because it is undoable.

At this point, John and Russell had accumulated five pieces of misinformation:

1. Don't feel bad.
2. Replace the loss.
3. Grieve alone.
4. Just give it time.
5. Be strong for others.

There are many ideas that are not helpful for grievers. The five we have listed so far represent those with which you will probably identify. While not absolute, they have a universality to them. This next one is also so common that most people believe it to be true and helpful, yet it is neither.

"You have to keep busy," or, "You must stay active," are two of the clichés that we have all heard following any kind of significant loss.

**Meaning: Keep busy.**

Here is an important question. Does keeping busy discover and complete the pain caused by loss? The obvious answer is no. Then what does keeping busy accomplish, if anything? It distracts you. It makes one more day go by.

Keeping busy buries the pain of the loss under an avalanche of activity. Every griever we have ever talked to will say, "No matter how busy I stay, at the end of the day, there's still a hole in my heart."

In addition to exhausting you, there are other dangers in keeping busy. Earlier we defined grief as "the conflicting feelings caused by the end of or change in a familiar pattern of behavior." A death, a divorce, or any other major loss produces massive changes in all things familiar. It is very difficult to adapt to life after a loss. If you were never a busy person before a loss, keeping busy would add yet another major change to the familiar.

The most dangerous flaw of keeping busy is the idea that it will make you feel better. Busy-ness is just a distraction. It does not alter the fact that you have to take direct actions to complete the pain caused by loss. We have heard this lament thousands of times: "I don't understand, I kept busy, but I felt worse, not better."

John and Russell and perhaps many of you were sent into life with several pieces of misinformation about dealing with loss. The six we have identified so far are:

1. Don't feel bad.
2. Replace the loss.
3. Grieve alone.
4. Just give it time.
5. Be strong for others.
6. Keep busy.

None of these ideas leads us to the actions of discovering and completing the unfinished emotions that accrue in all relationships.

## PARTICIPATING IN YOUR OWN RECOVERY

Earlier we talked about the fact that grievers have been taught to isolate themselves. You have probably experienced such isolation yourself. Since isolation is one of the problems confronting grievers in our society, then participation is clearly part of the solution.

To encourage you to participate in your own recovery, we are going to suggest that you start right now. Using the list of six incorrect ideas as a guide, see if you can think of any other ideas that you were taught or that influenced your beliefs about dealing with sad, painful, or negative feelings.

## LOSS OF TRUST

It is normal and natural to feel sad when a sad event happens. But every time we express our normal and natural responses, we are met with one or more of that list of false ideas, starting with, "Don't feel bad."

John and Russell each brought many of their painful emotional experiences to their parents, teachers, coaches, or others, only to be met with intellectual replies. The accumulation of unhelpful reactions began to add up to a loss of trust. While their initial loss-of-trust incident might have been with a parent or other adult authority figure, eventually the blanket of mistrust covered all relationships.

John's father was an alcoholic. When his father was intoxicated, he repeatedly spanked John for things he did not do.

> *Even though I would tell him it wasn't my fault, he didn't believe me and punished me anyway. It seemed very unfair to me, and my faith in him was diminished.*

Since the loss was never acknowledged or settled, John's suspicion of adults expanded. He trusted less and was on guard more. This limited John's aliveness and freedom. It limited the type of people with whom he could have trusting relationships. It caused him to be wary of all authority figures.

"I'm not saying that this general loss of trust was right on my part." Loss of trust was painful, so John learned that the solution was *don't trust,* thereby eliminating the potential for pain.

John's breakup with his first girlfriend reinforced the idea of not trusting people. From that point on, he found he had great difficulty in trusting the girls he dated. He was tentative and held back, since he didn't want to be hurt again. That attitude limited his capacity for aliveness. We know many grievers who have trouble starting up new relationships because they're afraid of enduring another loss. Most of you bought this book because of an awareness that something was not finished in your relationship to a death, a divorce, or another loss. Or you may have been given this book by a well-meaning friend or relative.

As this book unfolds, and as you participate in the actions that lead to recovery, you may recognize a sense of diminished trust. We cannot command you to feel safe or trusting about your feelings. We can, however, suggest that we too have been there. We did not feel safe either. We had been so conditioned to convert our emotions into intellect that we thought we were defective for having feelings at all. Please keep reading, even if you don't trust right now.

## PRACTICE MAKES HABITS

Why do we persist in trying to use information that hasn't worked for us? To understand why, you need to know some things about the computer we call the mind.

First, the mind has access only to what it has learned. It cannot use what it doesn't know. If you are given only misinformation, that's all you have access to. Second, the information stored in the mind is stored with importance attached. That means that the more important the source of the information, the more tenaciously we believe it to be right. Most of the data John and Russell acquired about loss came from their parents. To a child, parents are a very important source of information. Third, the mind's job is to believe that whatever it has stored in it is *always right!* This is why people are so critical of each other. If you believe you're right and others don't agree with you, then they must be wrong!

It's for these reasons that we persist in using misinformation in trying to process the feelings caused by loss. We believe that what we already know about loss is right. The fact that you are reading this book implies that what you have practiced is not delivering the relief and sense of well-being you want and deserve.

If you will accept the simple premise that you practiced and habituated some incorrect ideas, then you can allow that if you practice some correct ideas, you will have different results. We will give you correct information to help you discover and complete what is unfinished between you and others, living or dead. You must take action and practice what you learn here.

# 4

# Others Are Ill Prepared to Help Us Deal with Loss

In reading chapter 3, you probably identified with some of the experiences described. You may have recognized some of your own early life experiences in which you learned to process loss incorrectly. Almost everyone in our society has some kind of inadequate and inappropriate information stored in the computer of their mind.

It is only natural and quite healthy for people who are caught in a grieving situation to seek solace from those around them. However, in rather short order it becomes abundantly clear to the griever that friends and associates are not of much help. Even though they are well meaning, they often say things that can seem inappropriate.

## THEY DON'T KNOW WHAT TO SAY

Let's start with one of the common phrases heard by grieving people. Whether your loss was from death, divorce, or any other major event, you may have heard, "I know how you feel." This is delivered with great compassion, and with intent to soothe.

Most people report that they are anything but soothed by that comment. If the comment is well intended, why do most grievers react strongly against it? The answer lies in the ultimate truth about grief and grief recovery mentioned earlier.

### All relationships are unique, no exceptions!

Therefore, no one knows how you feel.

*Even a well-meaning friend who has had a parallel loss does not know how you feel.* A similar loss is an intellectual fact. It is not emotionally helpful. It does not relate to the uniqueness of the individual relationship. The fact that my mother died and your mother died is nothing more than a shared intellectual fact. This personal fact is not much different or more important than our respective shoe sizes. If this sounds harsh, it is intentional. We must try to stop intellectual connections from overpowering emotional truths.

For example, if you had a warm and fuzzy, supportive relationship with your mom and I had a stormy, combative, painful relationship with my mom, do you "know how I feel?"

Let us repeat:

### All relationships are unique, no exceptions!

As you understand and accept this simple premise, you are well on the road to recovery. Recovery means "discovering and completing" what was unfinished for you in your "unique" relationship.

The great majority of well-meaning people around us do not have *successful* grief recovery experiences to share. Therefore, they unwittingly encourage us to *act recovered*. This phenomenon has become so common that our next chapter is devoted to it.

## THEY'RE AFRAID OF OUR FEELINGS

Very early on, society teaches us that having sad, painful, or negative feelings and showing them are somehow not appropriate. It starts with the admonition, "Big boys and girls don't cry." One can actually hear parents say, "Stop that crying or I'll give you a reason to cry."

Now, we don't want you to get the idea that parents are insensitive, because that isn't true. They only pass on to their children what they were taught. What they were taught was that sad, painful, or negative feelings and showing them are not acceptable in our society.

"Cry baby, cry baby" can be heard resounding around preschool playgrounds. This is proof that the lesson has already been learned by age four or five.

A small sample of the statements heard on a daily basis illustrates the fear that others have when we show our feelings.

"Get a hold of yourself."
"You can't fall apart."

"Keep a stiff upper lip."
"Pull yourself up by your bootstraps."

As a society, we're uncomfortable when confronted by displays of painful emotion. This all perpetuates a fear of showing the normal feelings that result from emotional loss.

## THEY TRY TO CHANGE THE SUBJECT

From time to time, you may have wanted to tell a friend how you were feeling about an important emotional event in your life. You might recall how your friend listened for a while and then said, "That sounds really bad, but have you been watching what's been going on in the stock market?"

This example, while typical, does not explain what is really happening. Let's take another example and look at it closely:

A griever whose mother has died tries to communicate with a friend.

FRIEND: How are you doing?
GRIEVER: I'm heartbroken. I miss her so much.
FRIEND: Don't feel bad, she's not in pain anymore.

Look at this subtle change of subject. It is the griever who is sad, and the friend shifts to talking about the person who died. The implication is that if your loved one is no longer suffering, then you shouldn't be either.

We should note that the skills and tools used by the friend in this scenario are no better or worse than those of most people in our society. The friend has been socialized with the same false ideas that we all learned. The friend is lovingly trying to execute the training received over a lifetime.

This change-the-subject attitude was displayed on the ABC television program *20/20* in a show about grief caused by the death of a pet. The program was really well done and very sensitive to a griever's feelings. When the segment was over, the camera shifted back to Hugh Downs and Barbara Walters. Walters had started to get tears in her eyes. Her final remark before the commercial was, "Before I cry, let's change the subject."

The clear message to viewers was that showing feelings is not acceptable. In other words, "Let's deal with our feelings by changing the subject."

## THEY INTELLECTUALIZE

The attempt to shift from emotions to intellect is a dangerous and counterproductive thing to do with grieving people. Grief is, by definition, the emotional response to loss. The cause of the loss itself is intellectual, but the reaction to it is emotional.

That's not to say there is anything wrong with using our minds, but where is it written that we can't employ both intellect and emotions when they're called for? One of humanity's great gifts is the ability to demonstrate and communicate emotions. Yet society seems to place negative value on this gift.

Our reliance on intellect at the expense of feelings has reached epidemic proportions—particularly where grief is concerned. One reason is that the death of a loved one is not an everyday occurrence. If statistics are to be believed, we will each experience the death of a loved one every nine to thirteen years. Even when combined with other significant emotional losses, a major grief event occurs so infrequently that we never really get familiar with the experience. Because of our lack of personal knowledge, we continue the habit of dealing with loss based on misinformation. This habit leads to the unsuccessful conclusion of grief events. It is not surprising that people approach emotional pain intellectually. Since we rely on our minds every day, we're far more practiced at using them.

Based on the informal surveys we conduct at each of our seminars, an average of four out of five reactions that grievers hear following the loss of a loved one imply that they shouldn't deal with the feelings they are experiencing. The things they hear usually appeal to the intellect. Researchers have studied the statements typically heard by grievers very shortly after a death. Many of these comments are so common that they have been identified and can be divided into two categories: (1) those that are helpful to grievers and (2) those that are not. The unhelpful comments are all well-meaning but invariably appeal to the intellect or give advice that is difficult or dangerous to follow, such as:

> "Be thankful you have another son."
> "The living must go on."
> "He's in a better place."
> "All things must pass."
> "She led a full life."
> "You'll find somebody else."
> "God will never give you more than you can handle."
> "Be grateful you had him for so long."

These are all comments that we ourselves as grievers have heard. Since the griever is experiencing intense emotional suffering, these statements, which all have to do with the intellect, are quite inappropriate. Divorce and other significant emotional losses generate similar unhelpful comments from well-meaning friends.

## THEY DON'T HEAR US

Let's not limit the discussion to the comments heard following a death or divorce. The following situation, which has nothing to do with death or divorce, illustrates how incorrectly others often respond to our normal feelings. One of our friends was having a party. Her teenage daughter, Mary, had invited three of her best friends to the event. As the party was starting, the phone rang several times. The three best friends each called to say they had made other plans. Mary was very upset. She went to her mom and told her what had happened. Mom said, "Don't feel bad, there are a lot of nice people here to enjoy." Do you remember that when John's dog died, and when his grandpa died, the first response was always, "Don't feel bad." Here we go again—don't feel the way you feel, because sad, painful, or negative feelings are no good. You must find a more acceptable feeling, something positive.

Fortunately, a close friend of the family was standing nearby. Mary decided to take another chance at getting someone to hear what she was saying. She told the friend what had happened. He listened and then responded: "Ouch, you must be *so* disappointed." "Yes," she sobbed. He hugged her. She thanked him for listening, went and cleaned up her face, and then enjoyed the party, *after* her feelings were heard and acknowledged.

Grieving people want and need to be *heard*, not fixed. In this true story, the family friend didn't repair anything; he merely heard the emotion being communicated. That was all

Mary needed. She could then make the intellectual decision to enjoy the balance of the evening even though it was not going to be exactly as she had envisioned it. To a certain degree, effective grief recovery is about being heard.

## THEY DON'T WANT TO TALK ABOUT DEATH

Another form of distraction is how people talk, or don't talk, about death. In fact, we've gone to such extremes to avoid talk about death that some of us can't even say the word *death*. Think about it:

> "She passed away."
> "He's gone to his eternal rest."
> "Dad's gone."
> "He expired."
> "We've lost Mother."

Imagine how all this sounds to small children, who expect to hear truthful answers.

> *What happened to Grandpa?*
> *Grandpa's gone to sleep.*

The child takes one look at Grandpa in the casket and knows something isn't quite right about that answer. He's confused but assumes he's been told the truth. There must be two types of sleep. So he then spends the next six months being afraid to go to sleep at night.

We're sorry to say this, but God has been given a bad name where children are concerned.

> *What happened to my daddy?*
> *God has called him home.*

For the next several years, the child is upset and confused by God. Don't you think it might be more appropriate to tell the child what the parents believe to be the truth? "Your dad has died. And we believe that after he died, he went to be with God."

**Generally, it is best to avoid all metaphors when speaking about death with children. Developing young minds do not always have the ability to match reality with metaphorical images.**

## PROFESSIONAL DISTORTIONS

Our beliefs establish how we feel. If we have false ideas, we are liable to generate false feelings. The particular area that seems to have been the most shrouded in incorrect ideas is grief, so much so that the word *grief* is often replaced by inaccurate and confusing words.

When a loss occurs, a person experiences grief. Grief is the entire range of naturally occurring human emotions that accompany loss. When grief is incorrectly defined, a griever is unwittingly discouraged from following the normal sequence of emotions and actions that could lead to recovery. Grief is the normal and natural reaction to loss. Of itself, it is neither a pathological condition nor a personality disorder. Pressure, burnout, stress, PTSD (post-traumatic stress disorder), or

ADD (attention deficit disorder) are some of the false labels applied to grief. Those words have meaning and value when used in their correct context. But they become dangerous and misleading when misused.

Perhaps the most misused and misunderstood word on the topic of grief is *depression*. Tragically, it is the incorrect use of this one word that has engendered an epidemic of pharmacological intervention in grief.

We want this book to be helpful, without reading like a textbook. To keep this as simple as possible, let us give you an idea of what we mean. Clinical depression, as defined by a psychiatrist or psychologist, includes many of the same symptoms that a grieving person might report following a death or divorce. When grievers use the word *depression,* they typically are signifying "a lowered state of feeling or energy." Let's say someone's spouse of forty years has died. Doesn't a lowered level of energy seem logical? Isn't the griever entitled to some diminished feelings as he or she adapts to the painful and confusing new reality? We think so.

Many people have been conditioned to seek a medical solution to a nonmedical problem. This can be dangerous. Treatment of grief in the form of psychotropic drugs can hide the normal and natural reactions to loss. Once buried, it is difficult to reconnect those feelings at a later date.

From a grief recovery perspective, drug therapies fall into the general category of short-term energy-relieving behaviors (STERBs). There is no doubt that drugs have the capacity to divert and distract. In certain circumstances, an individual can derive some short-term benefit from the use of low-dosage mind-altering drugs. The danger is in the illusion of well-being that often accompanies such treatment. This illusion may lead to long-term dependence on the drugs.

You may feel substantial pressure from professionals and family members to begin drug treatment in response to loss. Try to remember that they too were socialized in the same world that taught us to respond to feelings with substances. "Don't feel bad, have some milk and cookies, you'll feel better." Be alert to the parallel idea, "Don't feel bad, have a pill, you'll feel better."

We know that during this vulnerable time you may have difficulty making reasoned decisions. We suggest that you try to accept the naturally occurring pain caused by your loss and attempt the program of recovery outlined in this book. If you find it too difficult, you can always use the drugs as a second alternative.

We are not promoting pain. If there were a softer, easier way, we would tell you about it. Grief is painful. It is supposed to be. Our experience shows clearly that approaching grief naturally has much more long-term benefit than any other option.

## THEY WANT US TO KEEP OUR FAITH

In 1969 John's younger brother died. John remembers being told, "You shouldn't be angry with God."

John knew he shouldn't be angry with God, but he was anyway. No one knew to tell him that anger at God is a typical response to an untimely death. We've relied on intellect for years, so we search for understandable reasons for events. When we can't find a reason, we assign blame to God.

This anger will pass if we're allowed to express the feeling. We have to be allowed to tell someone that we're angry with God and not be judged for it, or told that we're bad because of it. If not, this anger may persist forever and block spiritual growth. We've known people who never returned to their religion because they weren't allowed to express their true feelings. If this happens, the griever is cut off from one of the most powerful sources of support he or she might have.

## Faith and Feelings: There Is a Difference

Over the past several years, we have found it helpful to ask grievers to distinguish between faith and feelings. We realize that may sound like a strange idea, but most people sense what we mean by it. We have been discussing emotions and intellect. Now we need to address the spiritual aspect of grief. While it may be possible to find a direct cause-and-effect linkage between intellectual thoughts and the feelings that follow, faith is different. Faith does not require reason. It is spiritual, not emotional or intellectual.

There are two very distinct probabilities following a loss: (1) your religious or spiritual faith may be shattered or shaken, or (2) regardless of the nature of the loss, your faith is undamaged.

It is most often the death of a child or a sudden tragic accident that creates a major breach in a person's faith. We suggest that the griever work first on his or her relationship with the person who died. After completing the pain caused by that loss, faith usually returns naturally, and often with renewed intensity. If faith does not return, we help people heal their loss of trust in God. We use the same principles to complete loss-of-trust experiences with parents, doctors, clergy, and therapists.

For those whose faith is not damaged, we encourage them to use the power of their faith to give them the courage to take the actions of grief recovery. Again, to use the metaphor of the flat tire, here are two choices: (1) to sit down in front of the flat tire and pray for God to cause air to get back in, or (2) to call the automobile club, then pray to God to have the auto club get there quickly.

Unresolved grief is always about undelivered emotional communications that accrue within a relationship over the course of time. Faith and prayer are wonderful tools to apply to daily living. However, faith and prayer do not, of themselves, discover and complete what is unfinished.

In religious terms, it is said that God helps those who help themselves. We agree. We believe that helping ourselves is taking the actions of grief recovery—discovering and completing what is unfinished for us in our relationships.

# 5

# Academy Award Recovery

In the last chapter, we mentioned the fact that society literally teaches us to *act recovered*. Understanding this aspect of grief is enormously important. A false image of recovery is the most common obstacle all grievers must overcome if they expect to move beyond their loss. *Academy award recovery* is its name. It could also be called "I'm fine," or, "Put on your happy face," or, "Be fine for my family and friends," or, "I want to help others." You might sit down and ask yourself how many of these "act-recovered" faces you're currently using. Most of you already know what we're talking about.

In the previous chapter, we discussed how those around the griever respond at the time of a loss. We showed that the vast majority of comments a griever hears appeal to the intellect and do not encourage the expression of feelings. Such intellectualizing increases a griever's sense of isolation and creates a feeling of being judged, evaluated, and criticized. In a relatively short time, the griever discovers that he or she must indeed "act recovered" in order to be treated in an acceptable manner.

## ENSHRINE OR BEDEVIL?

In an attempt to be accepted and to look recovered, grievers try to focus on only fond memories. Where incomplete grief is concerned, this is known as "enshrinement." Enshrinement, in its most damaging form, can include obsessively building memorials to the person who died. This can be demonstrated by keeping large numbers of objects that represent the person. An example is the mother who did not change one item in her daughter's room although her daughter had been dead for more than five years.

Less critical but equally limiting is the enshrinement that simply doesn't allow the griever to look accurately at all aspects of the relationship. Many grievers limit their thoughts and feelings to fond memories or positive comments about the deceased. The idea that "you must not speak ill of the dead" is an example of unhelpful information. We do not suggest that anyone run around badmouthing anybody, living or dead. We do suggest that it's almost impossible to complete the pain caused by death, divorce, or other significant emotional loss without looking at everything about the relationship, not just the positive.

Bedevilment is the opposite of enshrinement. The griever has a litany of complaints detailing a lifetime of mistreatment. They are unwilling to let go of disappointments and anger. With bedevilment, the griever clings to the negatives just as the enshriner clings to the positives, but neither views the entire relationship.

**All relationships include both positive and negative interactions. We know that you can complete grief only by being totally honest with yourself and others.**

## WE WANT THE APPROVAL OF OTHERS

We all like praise and compliments. We all like approval. We all want to be seen as smart, strong, and mature. We all want to feel as if we are part of the group. This need is learned during early childhood and often reinforced to the point of obsession.

Earlier we mentioned that a large percentage of the comments made to grieving people following a loss are not helpful. Grievers are advised to take actions that merely distract or to convert feelings into intellectual ideas. Since approval is such a powerful aspect of our social skills, we try to conform to the ideas suggested to us following a loss.

When John's infant son died, it tore him apart. What he heard, however, were comments such as:

> "You and your wife should be grateful that you can have other children."
> "It was just not meant to be."
> "You're strong enough to handle it."

While intellectually all these statements were true, they still didn't help John to deal with his feelings. John sensed that his friends didn't want to hear about his feelings. But he didn't want to be alone. The question was, how could he honestly share his feelings without driving listeners away?

When Russell and his first wife divorced, well-meaning friends said:

> "You'll do better next time."
> "She wasn't right for you."

Russell had a normal need to be heard. But those comments stopped him from talking and inadvertently encouraged him to bury his feelings.

John and Russell both wanted the approval of those around them. They were tired of feeling bad, but they did not feel supported by their family and friends in their attempts to feel better. So they opted for academy award recovery. They began to put on their academy award faces even though they were not recovered by any stretch of the imagination. Their performances were so good that they nearly convinced themselves that they were all right when they were not.

## "I'M FINE" IS OFTEN A LIE

Through our work with grievers around the country, we get to see some of the most put-together people on Earth. They look good, they sound good, and they even try to convince us they are feeling good. When we meet people who've just experienced a loss, we ask them how they're doing. Invariably, the answer is the same: "I'm fine."

When we make speeches to large groups, we often ask how many people like being lied to. Of course, no one raises their hand. Then we ask how many of them have lied about their feelings following sad or painful events. All of the hands go up. It is very sad when you realize that we have been taught to lie about our feelings for fear of being judged or criticized.

The danger of "I'm fine" is that it does not help the broken heart. Saying "I'm fine" merely distracts us and others, while pain and loneliness persist on the inside. The net effect is to create a scab over an infection, leaving a mess underneath.

## WE BEGIN TO EXPERIENCE
## A MASSIVE LOSS OF ENERGY

In talking with thousands and thousands of grievers, we have rarely had a griever argue with us when we say that it sounds like they just don't have any energy left. Sometimes it is all a griever can do to get out of bed and go through the motions of a day, a week, a month, and eventually a lifetime on automatic pilot, with almost no energy.

Unresolved grief consumes tremendous amounts of energy. Most commonly, the grief stays buried under the surface, and *only the symptoms are treated.* Many people, including mental health professionals, misunderstand the fact that *unresolved loss is cumulative and cumulatively negative.*

It is reasonable to suggest that human energy is used most efficiently when our minds and bodies are in harmony. Unresolved grief tends to separate us from ourselves. As an example, how many times have you been driving down the road and then suddenly realized that for the last three blocks you were anywhere but driving the car? You were in your head, having a conversation with someone who was not in the car. And it's a miracle that you're still alive. Quite often those phantom conversations are with someone who has died or with a former spouse. More likely than not, these conversations represent an aspect of unfinished emotional business between you and someone else, living or dead. Holding on to incomplete emotions consumes enormous amounts of energy.

## WE EXPERIENCE A LOSS OF ALIVENESS

As a direct result of living in the deception of academy award recovery, many people experience a kind of false recovery based on their convincing performance. This can lead to a loss of aliveness and spontaneity that is almost impossible to overcome. Many people fall into a trap of quiet desperation—sometimes feeling good, sometimes feeling bad, but never being able to return to a state of full happiness and joy.

We pay a high price for the incorrect information we have about dealing with loss. Each time a loss is not properly concluded, there is cumulative restriction on our aliveness. Life becomes something to endure; the world seems like a hostile place in which to live. Because of misinformation, we never had a fair chance to deal effectively with the loss events in our lives.

Some of you are reading this book for reasons other than death or divorce. You might reflect upon your childhood; life was going to be happy and joyous. But owing to many small but unresolved losses over time, you may have awakened one day to find that life had just not worked out the way you hoped it would.

Some of you may not even remember having the idea that life was going to be wonderful. For you, there may be a cumulative sense that your life is not happy—but discontent is all you know. You may have very little or no reference point for joy.

In either case, you may have tried in many ways to improve your sense of happiness and well-being. Therapy, religious or spiritual beliefs, or twelve-step programs may have contributed valuable insights and tools. And yet, you may have a lingering sense that you are incomplete with your past, a feeling that, in turn, diminishes your hopes about the future.

Please do not stop now. This book is for you too.

# PART TWO

## *Preparing for Change: Starting to Recover*

Recovery from loss is achieved by a series of small and correct choices made by the griever. You have already made several correct choices:

> You have acknowledged that a problem exists.
>
> You have acknowledged that the problem is associated with loss.
>
> You have acknowledged, by beginning to read this handbook, that you are now willing to take action to complete your grief.

The next four chapters will introduce you to the first actions necessary for moving beyond loss. Success in moving through grief depends on your willingness to follow through on each action along the way.

# 6

# Your First Choice:
# Choosing to Recover

To make the choice to recover, we need to know where and how to begin. There are three words that help us begin the process of recovery: *different, better, or more.*

Whether the loss is a death, a divorce, or a painful estrangement from another person, the question "What do you wish had been *different, better, or more?*" will always help you find what is incomplete.

Let's go back to John's story from the day his grandfather died.

When John was sent to the principal's office to be alone, it reinforced the lesson he'd been taught all of his life about not talking about his feelings. As John sat in the office and reflected on the relationship, he wanted to thank his grandfather for all he had learned from him. John had often put off expressing his feelings until a later date. Before "later" arrived, his grandfather died. John was stuck with the undelivered "thank you." This was one of the things he wished had been *different, better, or more.*

John started to feel bad about the choices he had made. Many people in our world mistakenly call this guilt. Wishing that things could somehow have been **different, better, or more** is not the same as feeling guilty.

If we do not identify *different, better, or more,* we begin to make the death or other loss responsible for how bad we feel. As long as we believe that someone or something else is responsible, we're unable to recover.

## WHO IS RESPONSIBLE?

After recognizing the fallacy that "grief just takes time," the next most difficult hurdle for grievers to overcome is the incorrect belief that other people or events are responsible for their feelings. Many have a tendency to say:

> "So-and-so made me angry."
> "So-and-so ruined my day."
> "I'd be okay if So-and-so hadn't done such-and-such to me."

This attitude of nonresponsibility for our feelings and our actions is rampant. This too starts with early "influence learning."

> Mom says to the child, "You make me happy."
> Dad says, "You make me proud."
> Mom says, "Don't make your daddy mad."

As the direct result of being told that their actions cause feelings in Mom or Dad, children realize that the opposite must also be true. *If I can make Mom or Dad feel something, then they can make me feel something.* This is a major contribution to the "victim" mentality that has crept into so many areas of modern life.

To paraphrase Eleanor Roosevelt, *no one can make you feel bad about yourself without your permission.* But even with the help of that very accurate statement, we find it increasingly difficult to dissuade people from the belief that others are responsible for their feelings. When we make other people or events 100 percent responsible for causing our feelings, then we also make them responsible for ending our feelings.

There's a story we've often used to illustrate this concept. We call it the "on the way to work in the car" story.

> *One morning a man is on his way to work in his car. He comes to a red light, and being a law-abiding person, he stops. Sitting at the light, he begins to daydream. Meanwhile, the light changes from red to green. Our friend doesn't see the light change; the driver in the car behind him does. When our friend's car doesn't move, the guy behind him sounds his horn to notify him that the light has turned green. Our friend then rolls down his window and thanks the guy behind him for honking at him and calling his attention to the fact that the light has changed.*

Whom are we kidding here? We all know that it goes more like this.

> *Our friend becomes embarrassed. No one likes to feel embarrassed. He sure doesn't want to be responsible for causing his own embarrassment. He too has a lifetime's practice of making others responsible for his feelings. So, instead of saying "Thank*

*you" to the driver for calling his attention to the fact that the light has changed, he thinks: "Boy, that guy makes me mad!"*

Almost at once, his mind becomes filled with plans and schemes to save face or get even. He rolls down his window, puts his head out, and does exactly what he learned to do in that self-help seminar he attended two years before. He reports his feelings: "Hey, buddy, get off my back!"

*He then proceeds to drive a little bit slower in front of this guy in order to punish him for ruining his day. He knows he's right about this one!*

Our friend is angry and cannot see that he is the architect of his own discomfort. He doesn't acknowledge that he is indeed responsible for the feelings that result from his attitudes and actions.

What ruins the picnic—the rain or one's attitude about the rain? This is a trick question. The answer is both. The rain really does ruin the picnic, but you cannot do anything about the rain, you can only deal with your reaction to the rain. The same is true of almost all losses. What causes my grief—the loss or my reaction to the loss? Again, the answer is both. While we cannot undo what has happened, we can do something about our reaction. We can acquire skills to help us complete our relationship to the pain, disappointment, frustration, and heartache caused by what has happened.

Some people are ready to believe that a late bus or a serving of cold eggs is the result of an international conspiracy. Others think that the government is ruining their lives, or that the boss is the cause of their misery. But what this all boils down to is the belief that "they make me angry." This leads to an almost automatic critical response toward anyone or anything we misperceive as being responsible for our feelings. We become expert at *other*-examination rather than *self*-examination.

**As children, we could not change the actions of parents and other adults. Sometime after our childhood, we may become aware of events that happened before we had the power to alter them. We must take responsibility for our *current reaction* to what happened in the past. Otherwise, we will forever feel like a victim.**
**It is bad enough that horrible things happened to us. It becomes diabolical when we ourselves sustain and re-create the pain through our own memories. The problem is heightened by the fact that we were not taught correct skills to complete the pain caused by the memories of long-ago events.**

We have been falsely socialized to believe that we are victims of events and helpless in our responses to those events, as well as to the thoughts, feelings, and actions of others. Therefore, we inevitably believe that the rain is exclusively responsible for our disappointment. Most people are advised to just "let it go" or told that "what's done is done." It would be ideal if the human brain and human heart could simply dismiss problems and move on. But it does not work that way. Nothing can change until you take responsibility for your own recovery. To assist you in breaking the habit of feeling 100 percent a victim of a loss, we are going to ask you to adopt a new idea. We ask you to take 1 percent responsibility for your part of what is incomplete. Inasmuch as a small key can unlock a large door, 1 percent responsibility can open your head and your heart to the path of recovery. For now, that means continuing to turn the pages so you can find the solution.

## YOUR SECOND CHOICE: PARTNERSHIP OR WORKING ALONE

In a perfect world, the process of grief recovery would occur in a group setting. The stimulus of many people's stories helps others create accurate memory pictures of their own losses. If you are reading this book, it may be because you have no direct access to one of our Grief Recovery Seminars or Grief Recovery Outreach Programs.

In the first edition of *The Grief Recovery Handbook*, readers were told that recovery from loss could not be achieved alone, that they had to have a partner. Sadly, many people saw that and put the book down. As a result, they did not take the actions that lead to recovery from significant emotional loss. Since that time, we have discovered that recovery is always possible, even if you're working alone.

### For Those Working Alone

If circumstances and events in your life make it unrealistic or too fearful for you to have a partner, then *take the actions in this book alone*. Don't stop now.

We will present the applicable instructions for your grief recovery actions whether you are working with or without a partner.

**Partners**

We still believe that, *if you have a choice*, it is best to have a partner, someone who is working on their own loss. As a rule, they would be working on a different loss than you. However, following a death, it is not uncommon for family members to be partners. They might even work on the same loss. But since every relationship is unique, the recovery will also be unique. It is also perfectly okay within a partnership if one person is working on a death and the other on a divorce or some other loss.

## FINDING A PARTNER

You may feel that no one really understands the pain you're in. You may feel that even your own friends don't really comprehend your sorrow. When people say they understand, they really can't. They didn't have the same relationship that you had. Even other family members had their own special relationships.

Grievers are often told to seek others who have experienced a similar loss. Widows are told they can relate only to widows; parents who have lost children are told they can relate only to other such parents. This is false. We have found that anyone who has suffered intense emotional loss can become an ideal partner.

It may be that another family member is grieving over the same death. If you haven't clearly expressed how you're feeling, he or she may not know. You may already have a built-in partner for your recovery work in your own family.

If not, there are countless places to look for such a new friend. At work, you've heard people talk about someone who died. Your local health club, the grocery store, and your religious or social organization are all places where you can find another griever. Bring up the topic of grief at a social gathering. Everyone has a story. They may be thrilled to discover that a program of recovery is available.

When you do find potential partners, be honest with them. Show them this book and tell them what you plan to do. Ask whether they're tired of hurting too. See whether they're willing to recover with you. Don't be discouraged if several choose not to. You'll hear all kinds of excuses. Just keep looking until you're successful.

# 7

# *Setting the Guidelines*

In this chapter, we presume that you have either found a partner or chosen to work alone. Here are the specific guidelines for the initial partner meeting. *Even if you are working alone, read this part.* Some of the commitments and instructions, as noted, are also for you.

## INITIAL PARTNERS MEETING

Your first meeting will not require a great deal of time. An hour should be enough. There will be five more meetings to process the actions outlined in this book. You will probably need at least two or three days between meetings to complete reading and homework assignments.

At this first meeting, establish which day or night works best for both of you. You will probably want to allow at least an hour and a half or two hours for all subsequent meetings.

Make sure you *always* choose a place that will be safe.

Talking about your losses will probably generate some normal and natural human emotions, which may be accompanied by tears. Crying is normal and natural, especially in response to thoughts or discussions about grief. But crying is not essential. Do not decide that you or your partner are defective if there are no tears. By the same token, do not put a false value on tears. Crying is not completion. One of you make a commitment to supply tissues.

Establish within your partnership whether hugs are safe for both of you. Some people do not wish to be hugged. Let that be okay. Also, as a rule, do not hug or touch your partner in the middle of an exercise. Wait until the end. Often physical touch stops a feeling that might otherwise be helpful.

In general, we suggest that you sit a reasonable distance apart, so that the person talking does not feel smothered or intimidated. Try to think of yourselves as friends having a conversation. *This is not therapy.* The topic may seem awkward at first, but the goal is to feel comfortable and safe talking about loss. We suggest that you think of yourself as a *heart with ears* as you listen to your partner.

## MAKING COMMITMENTS

You must make certain commitments if the grief recovery process is to work for you.

1: *Total Honesty* (for both partners and those working alone). When we say total honesty, we mean that you should be honest to the best of your ability about the loss events in your life and your feelings about them. Your ability to see and therefore tell the truth about these things will improve as you continue to work in this program. Total honesty means telling the truth *about yourself*, not about anyone else. Don't slip into the trap of talking about someone else. You can tell the truth only about yourself. When it comes to others, you are only guessing.

In no way are we assuming that you, the reader, are a dishonest person. There may be some things that you would be unwilling to tell to a partner. The facts and details about certain events may be too difficult to expose. That's okay. It is more important that you tell the truth about your emotional response to the events. Of course, those of you working alone need to be absolutely honest with yourselves.

2: *Absolute Confidentiality* (for partners). During the course of the work you must do, you're going to talk about emotionally painful events and circumstances in your life. Absolute confidentiality means that you carry any personal information shared by your partner to the grave with you. Absolute confidentiality means you trust your partner to do the same. It means that you must never breach your partner's confidence.

3: *Uniqueness and Individuality* (for partners and those working alone). The third commitment is to the uniqueness and individuality of each person's recovery. Since every relationship is unique, each set of recovery communications is unique. And since every griever brings a unique set of beliefs to the process of recovery, it is essential that you not compare beliefs. Comparison often leads to minimizing or maximizing, not to the truth. No one's opinion about your grief or beliefs is important other than your own. The safety of your partnership and your individual recovery hinges on each of you being able to communicate your own thoughts and feelings without interruption, analysis, criticism, or judgment.

Whether working alone or with a partner, it is essential that you support your recovery with commitments to take the actions of this program seriously, and to do all of the assignments in a timely manner.

*Partners*: Make sure that you verbalize and acknowledge these commitments to each other.

*Those Working Alone:* You are only required to make the first commitment. However, it is especially important that you take it seriously. You are also advised to look at the third commitment, particularly the part about not being judgmental or critical of yourself.

## FIRST HOMEWORK ASSIGNMENT

Both partners and those working alone should read or reread the first six chapters of this handbook. Make notes and underline statements that affect you. Note things that you relate to from your own experience.

Here is the list of myths John and Russell had learned in dealing with the losses in their lives:

1. Don't feel bad.
2. Replace the loss.
3. Grieve alone.
4. Just give it time.

5. Be strong for others.
6. Keep busy.

Don't Talk about it

Don't be surprised if you relate to most or all of them. It is very common in our society to have been socialized with exactly these beliefs.

Using a clean sheet of paper, write down any of the six ideas to which you relate. Add any other ideas that you were taught or have observed in those around you in connection with loss events. This list will begin to personalize your recovery.

Next, review the following list of clichés. See how many of the comments you have heard and learned to believe. Again, don't be surprised if most or all of them sound familiar. These beliefs about grief are very common in our society. Add any other comments you may have heard in connection with loss events.

"Get a hold of yourself."
"You can't fall apart."
"Keep a stiff upper lip."
"Pull yourself up by your bootstraps."
"We understand how you feel."
"Be thankful you have other children."
"The living must go on."
"He's in a better place."
"All things must pass."
"She led a full life."
"God will never give you more than you can handle."
"You shouldn't be angry with God."

You sound stupid talking about it

This list represents many of the concepts, beliefs, and ideas that you have been trying to use in dealing with the losses in your life.

Even though this list seems long, we've rarely met anyone who could not add several variations to it. Please do not perceive this as a criticism of you, your family, your church, or society in general. It is essential that you identify which ideas you are using to deal with grief so that you can see whether they are helping or hindering your recovery. Be thorough. The more truth you put into this exercise, the easier it will be for you to adapt to some better ideas of recovery later in this book.

## REVIEW THOUGHTS AND REMINDERS

Earlier we noted some false ideas that limit our ability to deal effectively with grief, including:

"Get a hold of yourself."
"You can't fall apart."
"Keep a stiff upper lip."
"Pull yourself up by your bootstraps."

We must always remind ourselves that grief is the *normal and natural* response to loss. Grief is a human response that lets us know that for the moment things are different than they were before the loss. These four comments imply that there is something *wrong* or *defective* about us when we react normally to loss events. Yet it is normal to be overwhelmed when an overwhelming event or series of events occurs. It is normal to feel lost, dazed, confused, and frustrated when major losses affect our lives. It is common to hear that someone, in response to the emotion or as a reaction to loss, *broke down* or *lost it*. It is tragic that such incorrect language and ideas have poisoned our beliefs about dealing with the normal and healthy feelings associated with loss.

## SECOND PARTNERS MEETING

Begin by reaffirming your commitments to total honesty, absolute confidentiality, and the uniqueness of your individual recovery. As always, meet in a private place where you will not feel uncomfortable if you cry. Have tissues handy.

This meeting is your first real opportunity to determine what ideas you have been using to deal with all of the losses in your life. This meeting is the only one in which you will have a chance to talk in a general way about grief and loss and to discuss the things you have been led to believe. Later meetings will be more specific as you move toward completion.

There are three potential pitfalls. The first is a tendency to monologue rather than discuss. The second is to become analytical, critical, or judgmental. The third is to bring in ideas from religious, spiritual, intellectual, therapeutic, or twelve-step philosophies. While all of those arenas have substantial value in day-to-day living, their ideas are often confusing when applied to grief.

The objectives are to establish that each of you has substantial misinformation about dealing with loss and to create safety between you. Safety will help reduce isolation and increase participation. You may be surprised to see how much you have in common.

Each of you, in turn, will read your list of myths. These will be some or all of the six myths that John and Russell learned early in their lives. Spend some time discussing the impact those myths had on your life.

Then, taking turns, read your list of other ideas that illustrate the concepts and beliefs you have been using to deal with loss. Again, spend some time discussing the impact those myths have had on your life.

Make plans for your next meeting.

### For Those Working Alone

Set aside some time to reread the first six chapters. Review the lists you made and compare them with those in the book. Think about the impact they have had on your life and then jot down notes about that impact. Ask yourself this awkward question: "Am I working alone in part because of some of the beliefs I learned about dealing with painful feelings?"

# 8

## Identifying Short-Term
## Energy Relievers

The death of a loved one, divorce, and all other losses produce an incredible amount of emotional energy. Since we have all been socialized from early on to deal with sad, painful, and negative emotions incorrectly, we end up storing the energy inside ourselves.

The most clichéd of stories illustrates that fact. A little child comes home from preschool with her feelings hurt by interactions with the other children on the playground. Mom, Dad, Grandma, or any other caretaker says, "What happened?" The child responds, tearfully, that one of the kids was mean to her. The caretaker says, "Don't cry, here, have a cookie, you'll feel better," thus setting the child up with a lifetime belief, from an important authority source, that *feelings can be fixed with food.*

Upon eating the cookie, the child feels *different*, not better, and for the moment is distracted and forgets about the incident on the playground. However, there has been no completion of the emotional pain caused by the event. The event and the feelings attached to it are now buried under the cookie, the sugar, and the distraction. If the child were to bring it up sometime later, she would probably be told, "We don't cry over spilled milk," as if to say that it is not okay to continue having feelings about the incident. So it must stay buried.

Early on we learn to cover up, hide, or bury our feelings under food. It is not surprising that sometime later we adapt that same behavior and cover up our feelings under alcohol or other drugs. We may have learned to do so by observing family members at funerals or wakes consuming large amounts of food and alcohol. Consuming food or alcohol in response to the emotional energy created by death or divorce does not help us discover the source of the energy or complete the relationship affected by our loss. Therefore, we are participating in an *illusion* that the short-term relief offered by food or alcohol gives us long-term relief from the pain caused by the loss.

Food and alcohol are obvious and typical short-term energy-relieving behaviors. There are many, many other short-term behaviors that have the same life-limiting and damaging consequences. Here is a partial list of behaviors that, if done for the wrong reasons, can have a negative impact on grieving people:

- Food
- Alcohol/Drugs
- Anger
- Exercise
- Fantasy (movies, TV, books)
- Isolation
- Sex
- Shopping (humorously called retail therapy)
- Workaholism

Most of these actions are not harmful in and of themselves. They become harmful when you engage in them for the wrong reasons. Just as eating a cookie does not help the emotional pain of loss, shopping provides no long-term help for the pain caused by death or divorce. In fact, it can have quite the opposite effect: the shopping binge is often followed by remorse over the wasted money. This is a further distraction from the real and original emotional event—the death, divorce, or other loss.

While many short-term energy relievers are apparent, some are not. The following example illustrates another, more subtle danger.

It's not uncommon for people to visit grave sites on an extremely regular basis for years following a death. They feel as if the death robbed them of the chance to complete their emotional relationship, and so they often visit the place that best helps them feel close to their loved one. Unconsciously, these grievers are seeking some relief from the pain caused by the incomplete relationship. The problem is that visiting the grave doesn't lead to permanent relief or completion with the person who died.

At the end of this chapter, you will have an opportunity to look at how certain actions of your own may have been indirect ways of dealing with the feelings caused by loss.

## SHORT-TERM RELIEF DOESN'T WORK

Imagine a steam kettle filled with water. The flame under the kettle is turned up high. Normally, as the water heats and boils, the steam generated by the heat releases through the spout. Most kettles are fitted with a whistle to notify us when the water has reached the boiling point. Imagine that same steam kettle filled with water, with a high flame burning below and a cork jammed into the spout. Imagine the pressure that builds up inside that kettle when the spout cannot release the built-up energy. The cork represents a lifetime of misinformation that causes us to believe that we are not supposed to talk about sad, painful, or negative emotions.

A healthy steam kettle releases energy immediately as it builds up. When you are told, "Don't feel bad," and, "If you're going to cry, go to your room," the energy stays inside you. The myth that "time will heal" is laughable in terms of the steam kettle analogy. Time only moves the steam kettle closer to an explosion.

As the pressure builds up inside our personal steam kettle, we automatically seek relief. This is when we may start participating in the short-term energy relieving behaviors (STERBs) referred to in chapter 4. There are three major problems with STERBs. The first is that they work, or more accurately, they *appear* to work. They create an illusion of recovery by causing you to forget or bury emotions. The second problem with STERBs is that they are *short-term*. They do not last, and they do not deal with the true emotional issue. And lastly, they do nothing to remove the cork that is jammed in the spout. In fact, most people don't even realize that there *is* a cork in the spout.

Eventually, our steam kettle is overloaded and the STERBs no longer create the illusion of well-being. Imagine what might happen if a major loss event, a death or divorce, were added to this collection of unresolved emotions. It might put such a strain on our corked kettle as to cause an explosion.

While some emotional explosions are huge and make national headlines, most are much smaller. Here is an unfair question. Have you ever had an emotional explosion larger than circumstances called for? Sadly, we know that you all have to say yes. Over time, we develop the habit of putting a cork in our own personal steam kettles. We bottle up our feelings because we have been taught to do so.

The actions of grief recovery will help you remove the cork. You will then be able to deal more effectively with the emotions associated with loss. In order to remove the cork, we will look at all of the ideas that created it and replace them with more accurate ideas about dealing with sad, painful, and negative emotions.

A simple analogy: if your yard is full of weeds, you can cut the weeds to give some short-term relief, but they will grow back. Or you can pull the weeds and eliminate the problem. You are arriving at the point of making a decision: short-term or long-term relief. We want you to commit to long-term relief. And we will guide you and help you along the way.

## IDENTIFYING YOUR SHORT-TERM ENERGY-RELIEVING BEHAVIORS

Russell had never been much of a drinker. Even though he had been in the restaurant business most of his adult life, he rarely drank and never got drunk. Following his second divorce, he found himself going to a friend's bar and having one or two drinks every night. This behavior was reinforced by the friendliness at the bar. After about three months, this nightly ritual didn't seem to help anymore. He stopped drinking and started going home every night and reading escapist mystery novels. He substituted one short-term action for another. This was a classic example of short-term energy-relieving behavior.

## SECOND HOMEWORK ASSIGNMENT

The homework assignment (for both partners and those working alone) is to identify the short-term energy-relieving actions you have used or may be using to escape the pain caused by your losses.

After reading the chapter again, try to identify at least two examples of short-term relief you have used to displace your feelings. This is not as easy as it appears. It could be your first chance to demonstrate your commitment to total honesty.

Here is the list of short-term energy-relieving behaviors from earlier in the chapter. Use it as a guideline to help determine whether you have been relying on short-term relief.

- Food
- Alcohol/Drugs
- Anger
- Exercise
- Fantasy (movies, TV, books)
- Isolation
- Sex
- Shopping (humorously called Retail Therapy)
- Workaholism

Using a clean sheet of paper, write down the short-term energy relievers in which you have participated. Then add any others that you discover. It is actually very common in our society to have been socialized with the idea that we should cover up emotional pain rather than confront it directly.

## THIRD PARTNERS MEETING

Begin by reaffirming your commitments to total honesty, absolute confidentiality, and the uniqueness of your individual recovery. As always, meet in a private place where you will not feel uncomfortable if you cry. Have tissues handy.

Short-term energy-relieving behaviors (STERBs) can be a fun category for partners to talk about. However, it can also be painful and awkward. Be especially careful not to judge, criticize, or evaluate your partner (or yourself). Be mindful of your commitment to absolute confidentiality. Maintaining truth and safety is essential to recovery.

Read your list of STERBs. It is important to remember why we participate in them. It is not because we are defective, but because we were taught to do so.

One of the purposes of this exercise is to help you become aware of things that you may have been doing unconsciously. The possibility of changing some of the habits that hurt you lies in becoming aware that they exist.

After you have each had a turn, set the time and place for your next meeting.

### For Those Working Alone

Read the chapter again. Examine both the general and the specific ways in which you have used STERBs in your life to cope with loss.

Another awkward question: "Is it possible that one of my major short-term energy relievers is *isolation*? Is that another reason I'm working without a partner?"

It may seem like we are pressuring you. In fact, we are

sharing many years of experience. Most people who have difficulty finding a partner are merely afraid that a potential partner would refuse them. We cannot tell you that this would not happen, but please reconsider your choice of working alone. We will not mention this again.

# 9

# The Loss History Graph

Now that you've established that myths, intellect, and short-term energy-relieving behaviors have not been providing the kind of long-term benefits needed, you might have begun to feel stuck. This is the point at which you may have started to "act recovered." That's when you say, "I'm fine," when you really mean, "I'm hurting." This is a dangerous place to wind up.

If there were some magical way that we could lift the pain of your losses off your shoulders, we would. But we can't, so we'll do the next best thing. We will teach you how to complete your relationship to the pain caused by the loss.

The loss history graph is designed to help you discover what losses have occurred in your life and which of them are most restricting your day-to-day living. At first glance, it might seem strange for us to tell you that you need to identify the losses in your life. After all, shouldn't you know what they are? Sadly, many people, particularly when they were young, were taught to compare losses and minimize feelings. Thus, they may not be aware of the emotions they have from past events that continue to limit their lives.

## COMPARE AND MINIMIZE

Somewhere during your formative years, you heard the statement, "I cried because I had no shoes until I met a man who had no feet." Clearly, this statement is designed to get people to pause and be grateful for what they have rather than focus on what they don't have. While that is an admirable quality, it is often construed to mean, "Compare losses to minimize feelings."

Russell remembers a dinner party where he was seated next to two women friends. One woman's husband had died of cancer several months earlier. The other woman was in the middle of a painful divorce. Russell asked her how she was doing. She whispered, "Terrible, but I can't feel bad about my divorce because her husband died." This is a perfect example of compare and minimize.

## LOSS HISTORY GRAPH EXAMPLES

Once we establish a habit, we continue to use it unconsciously. Our lives are made up of many habits. You've probably been putting on the same shoe first all your life and never thought about it until right now. This is also probably true of how you've been trying to deal with the losses in your life. That's why a Loss History Graph is so important. We need to know what our pattern is so we can confront and change it.

The primary purpose of this exercise is to create a detailed examination of the loss events in your life and to identify the patterns that have resulted from them. There are several other reasons for making a Loss History Graph. One is to bring everything up to the surface where we can look at it. Buried or forgotten losses can extend the pain and frustration associated with unresolved grief. Another is to practice being totally truthful. We can often be dishonest without ever lying. That is, we omit things and thereby create an inaccurate picture. An additional benefit of using this exercise is observing which short-term relievers we have relied upon after losses.

We're all going to have other losses during our lives, and we don't want to fall into the same old traps. As the old mountain man told the young mountain man, "If you want to avoid bear traps, it's a good idea to know what they look like."

In order to do a Loss History Graph, it's a good idea to know what it looks like. Here are ours.

## JOHN W. JAMES

BORN: *February 16, 1944*

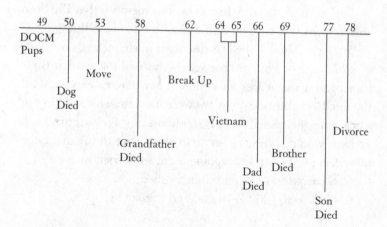

*'49 Puppies*—As a starting point, I'll tell you about my dawn of conscious memory. My first memory is from the day our family dog gave birth to a litter of puppies. Late one night, after my brother and I had gone to sleep, our father woke us up. He took us to the dog's bed. Our dog, who had always been friendly, seemed to be suspicious and wary. I remember being a little frightened. As my dad brought us closer to the bed, I could see three or four little lumps near her. Soon she began to whine and move around. I thought that she was in pain and wanted to help her. My father told us to stay back, that she was having trouble delivering one of the puppies. When he said that, it dawned on me what the little lumps were. I was happy, scared, proud, and confused all at the same time. Eventually, my father had to help her give birth to the last three puppies.

My brother and I wanted to hold and pet the puppies right away, but we were told that our dog might not like that, so we went back to bed. Of course, we couldn't sleep and spent half the night talking about this wondrous event. The next two weeks were spent being solicitous of our dog and waiting for the puppies to open their eyes.

This event is the very first conscious memory that I've been able to identify. I have no earlier recollection of anything.

*'50 Dog*—My dog died (as discussed in chapter 3).

*'53 Moving*—This was the year we moved for the first time. Moving is a major loss for children. My parents explained all the intellectual reasons why we were moving: we would live in a better neighborhood and a better house, it was closer to school, and we would own it rather than rent. That didn't make the move feel any better. I was going to miss my friends.

*'58 Grandfather*—My grandfather died.

*'62 Girlfriend*—My girlfriend and I broke up.

*'64/65 Vietnam*—The way Vietnam veterans were treated in our society reinforced the loss-of-trust experience. It is this loss of trust that causes so many problems for veterans even to this day. As a society, we have paid and are still paying dearly for this. During the years of the war, we suffered the deaths of more than fifty-eight thousand combat troops; in the years since the war ended, we have felt the loss by suicide of more than three times that number.

*'66 Father*—My father died. I had seen him only once since I came home from overseas; much was unfinished in our relationship. His drinking had continued until it finally killed him. It was a very painful experience for me.

*'69 Brother*—My younger brother, a twenty-year-old pole vaulter at Southern Illinois University, was in perfect health when he died. He was on his way to visit me in southern California, where I lived at the time. He was traveling with two of his friends from college; they'd stopped for the night and had all decided to take a nap. Later that afternoon, when his friends went to wake him, they found that he had died.

I spent days trying to find some intellectual reason for his death, and when I couldn't find one, I assigned blame for his death to God.

*'77 Son*—My son died. Two years earlier, my wife and I had had a daughter. Her arrival was the high point of my life. When my wife became pregnant again, I was looking forward to another such experience. About five months into the pregnancy, complications set in. When my wife went into premature labor, we raced to the hospital, where every possible medical technique was employed to slow or stop the process. She was hooked up to monitoring devices, and for two days we had to listen to a perfectly healthy heartbeat while knowing there was little chance the child would live.

All of my life I had been taught to believe certain things about what my job was as a man, a husband, and a father. I had been taught to believe that it was my job to identify problems and solve them. What I discovered right away was that it did not matter who I knew, what I knew, how much money I had, or how intelligent I was—there was nothing I could do. It was the most frustrating experience I had ever had.

Despite all the medical intervention, our son was born. For the first eight hours, it appeared that everything would be all right. Then things started to go wrong. Once again, identifying the problem was easy. I could see the problem: he weighed about two pounds, had black hair, and was encased in a glass box. But there was nothing I could do but stand and look at all the monitoring equipment and feel impotent.

This went on for two days. I was trying to help my wife because that was what I had been taught to do. There is nothing wrong with that except, in trying to help her, I was not acknowledging my own pain. At the end of the second day, my son just breathed out and never breathed in again.

If you can believe this, it started to go downhill from there. The things people said and did were shocking. That my wife and I were unable to talk became apparent. Our relationship began to fall apart immediately. During the next eight months, I went everywhere, talked to everyone, and read everything that I could get my hands on to help ease the pain. This was the point where I discovered there was little or no help available to deal with the grief. That was real despair.

*'78 Divorce*—My wife and I were divorced. The divorce happened because we had no idea how to deal with the grief caused by all the changes in our lives. We were newly married, new parents, and new grievers, all at the same time. The death of our son was the straw that broke the camel's back.

In typical griever fashion, my mind was preoccupied with thoughts of what I wished I had done *different, better, or more.* If I hadn't made the cost of medical bills such an issue, my wife might have gone for checkups more frequently. The night the emergency started, we had no baby-sitter and no real idea of the seriousness of my wife's condition, so I didn't go with her to the doctor's office. I used to sit and think about how frightening that must have been for her. Even as all of these thoughts were running through my mind, I had no skill or practice at being able to talk about what I was feeling. I felt isolated and alone, yet I truly believed that I was supposed to be strong and keep it all inside. Since that was all I knew, that is what I did. With that type of pressure building up, arguments became common. Hurt feelings were then added to the fire, and more arguments followed. At the same time, my wife was thinking that if she hadn't gotten pregnant so soon after the birth of our daughter, then none of this would have happened. That was her *different, better, or more* thinking. She too had no knowledge about the importance of talking about her feelings.

When communication breaks down in a marriage, no matter the cause, it is only a matter of time before divorce occurs. When the divorce takes place, we have yet another grieving experience to deal with, so the cycle continues.

While writing this book, I called my former wife to discuss her thoughts about telling this part of the story. One of the things she shared with me was the fact that she had not known for several years how much the death of our son affected me. How could she have possibly known? I was an academy award griever then.

Setting out to do a Loss History Graph can be a scary proposition. So before we ask you to do this exercise, we want you to see another example.

Here is Russell's loss history graph.

## RUSSELL FRIEDMAN

BORN: *January 4, 1943*

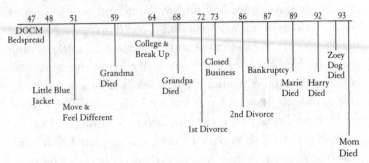

*'47 Dawn of Conscious Memory*—My first conscious memory is neither happy nor sad. It is a simple memory of a blue bedspread. It was covered with nautical designs.

*'48 Little Blue Jacket*—My father took me to a Rochester Royals basketball game. At the game, he bought me a Royals jacket. Some time later, I lost the jacket. When my father found out that the jacket was lost, he berated me for losing it. I remember feeling as if my father was no longer safe for me. After several other incidents of this type, I did not trust him anymore.

*'51 Feeling Different, Plus Major Move*—I was born allergic to milk, eggs, nuts, and chocolate. One of the consequences of the allergies was the need to have special food when I went to school. I felt very different from the other kids in my class. I also had very, very red hair, and approximately two and a half million freckles. That may sound cute. But as the possessor, it did not feel cute. I was teased often and sometimes cruelly by

the other children. I did not have the wherewithal to defend myself. I just felt so terribly different.

We lived in Rochester, New York, which gets very cold and damp in the winters. I suffered with asthma. It was so serious that my parents were advised to move to either Arizona or Florida for the heat. I did not want to leave my friends and the neighborhood to which I had grown accustomed. I made an emotional appeal to my parents. My appeal was met with intellectual explanations about a better school, a bigger house, and Daddy having a better job. My presenting emotions about my friends was never addressed.

We moved to Florida. In Florida, another physical problem surfaced that has had lifelong consequences. Having red hair and very light skin, Miami's intense heat and deadly ultraviolet rays had an immediate impact on my life. I was forced to wear shirts in the swimming pool and zinc oxide on my face so I could play outdoors. I suffered a few serious sunburns and also developed a fear of the sun. It started to affect my choice of activities, affecting in turn my friendships with my peers. The bottom line for me was that my red hair, fair skin, and freckles made me feel very *different* from everyone else.

*'57 Grandma*—Grandma died. She had been living with us since my mom had gone back to work. Grandma was the primary caretaker for my brother, who is ten years younger than me. This is where I learned to "be strong for others."

*'64 Broken Engagement*—This was my first full-fledged love affair, with major plans for marriage and children. When it crashed and burned, I was devastated. I had absolutely no ideas, tools, or skills to help me deal with the intense emotional pain. I was in my last year of college. I cut classes. I stared at walls. I just went through the motions.

*'64   College   Graduation*—Traditionally,   graduations   are perceived as positive experiences. And that is at least half true. I was torn, however, between the excitement and freedom of my new adult status and the sadness of leaving behind four years of people and places and familiarity. No one wanted to hear about or acknowledge the sad part.

*'68 Grandpa*—Grandpa died. I was not fond of my grandfather. He was very gruff, and I was scared of him. Even as I got older, I found his manner threatening. When he died, he and his son, my dad, had not been on good terms. I tried to "be strong" for my dad.

*'72 First Divorce*—This divorce was totally unexpected for me. I did not have an inkling that it might happen. I was devastated. I was confused. I was totally lost. The only tool I had for dealing with any kind of loss was "be strong for others." But this was me. *I was the other.* As I look back on it, I am amazed that I am still alive. I cannot imagine how I drove a car without accidentally killing myself or anybody else. It was almost impossible for me to concentrate. Even then, I knew that this loss was not singular. I had a sense that in addition to the loss of the marriage, there was the loss of all my hopes, dreams, and expectations, coupled with a massive "loss of trust." Since trust had always been a major problem for me, this divorce and how it happened crushed what little trust I had left.

*'73 Closed Business*—When my wife and I divorced, I kept the restaurant we had opened together. I was preoccupied with the emotions caused by the divorce. I had no effective skills for dealing with those painful emotions. While I had normally been a fairly attentive entrepreneur, my concentration was greatly diminished. I started making some very poor business decisions, which, in turn, led to poorer ones. In the

end, I closed the business down. My heart was not in it anymore.

*'86 Second Divorce*—This divorce was very different from the first one. The pain was intense. In addition to the death of the relationship and the hopes and dreams, another factor troubled me greatly. I was forty-three years old. My sense of myself, my life, and my future was different from what it had been after my first divorce. I was older. My business was in a neighborhood populated with elderly people. I used to sit and stare at the elderly couples, thinking, "When do I get to go off into the sunset with someone?" My parents and my wife's parents were still together. I was 0 for 2 in marriage. I felt like a complete failure.

*'87 Bankruptcy*—Having experienced a first divorce and closing a business in response to it did not prepare me for the second divorce and the financial tragedy that followed. In fact, the earlier events almost predicted the later ones. I was practiced at divorce, so I got another one. I was practiced at business failure, so I failed again. In neither case had I experienced recovery or completion of the emotions caused by the losses. The cumulative unresolved feelings created a massive preoccupation from which I made one horrible business decision after another. I had no alternative but to declare bankruptcy. Having been socialized to be the provider, the bankruptcy caused me to feel like the biggest "loser" on the planet.

*'89 Marie*—Marie, my girlfriend's mother, died. We had become quite close. I loved the way she asked me how I was doing and then really listened to my answer. By the time Marie died, I had begun working at the Grief Recovery Institute. More important, I had completed my relationship to the pain caused by the prior loss experiences in my life. My personal completions allowed two different things to occur.

First, I was as complete as I knew how to be with Marie while she was still alive. Second, I was really affected by her death. Having completed earlier relationships, my heart was open to new ones. Being open means that painful things hurt. That same openness had allowed me to be more loving. Sadness being the normal and healthy reaction to loss, Marie's death hurt my heart.

*'92 Harry*—Harry, my girlfriend's father, died. He and I had become very close after his wife, Marie, died. We spent countless hours on the couch at his house or my house watching every possible sporting event. He was eighty-seven, but he had an amazingly critical eye for all the details of each sport. He also had a wealth of knowledge of sporting events from before I was born. It was often like a fun history lesson for me. As fate would have it, Harry died just a few days before the Super Bowl. There was a very empty seat on my couch on Super Bowl Sunday.

*'93 Dog Zoey*—Our dog Zoey died. She was a 100-pound lap dog. (If a 100-pound dog wants to sit on your lap, you don't argue with her.) She was zany and wonderful, and as with many relationships with pets, mine with her was unconditionally loving. She had been with my girlfriend and her daughter since she was a puppy. When I moved in, she adopted me and trained me. When she got cancer, we tried everything, but to no avail. As I arrived home each evening shortly after she had died, my heart would fall to my feet as soon as the garage door started up. Those moments when I remembered that Zoey would not be at the top of the stairs to greet me were among the most painful I have experienced.

*'93 Mom*—The day before Thanksgiving, suddenly and unexpectedly, my mother died. Let me try to describe for you

what I experienced in the moments after I was told that she had died. I had walked into my office around 11:00 A.M., having just finished an early morning round of golf. As I walked through the office doorway, my assistant stood up and said, "Russell, I have terrible news, your mother has died!" I felt as if I had been hit in the chest with enough force to knock me down—my knees buckled and I started crying. As my legs sagged, my assistant and another friend surrounded me and held me up. I fell into their arms and sobbed and sobbed.

## WHAT GOES ON THE LOSS HISTORY GRAPH

Since most of us relate the words *grief* and *loss* primarily to death and perhaps to divorce, let's establish which human experiences come under the heading of grief. Here is the most helpful definition we use: *Grief is the conflicting group of human emotions caused by an end to or change in a familiar pattern of behavior.* Thus, any changes in relationships to people, places or events can cause the conflicting feelings we call grief.

Look at how many other loss events are also covered by this definition. Think about <u>moving</u>. When we move, every single familiar pattern may change. Where we live, where we work, and who we regularly see all change. Major <u>financial changes,</u> positive or negative, create massive changes in our familiar patterns. Major changes in bodily functions or abilities can have enormous grief consequences. Losing the use of limbs or eyesight or a condition like diabetes or kidney failure automatically alters familiar patterns. Strokes and heart attacks often affect how and when we exercise and what and when we eat. Menopause can cause huge feelings of loss for women as well as for their mates. <u>Divorce</u> is somewhat obvious when it is our own. We are also affected by the divorce of anyone we are close to—parent, child, sibling, or other.

<u>Childhood issues of</u> mistreatment—physical, sexual, or emotional—often set up patterns wherein positive interactions are sabotaged because they are not as "familiar" as negative interactions.

Many life experiences fit our definition of grief. Almost anything that has affected you negatively is a grieving experience for you. When you read John's and Russell's Loss History Graphs, you got some idea of which life events are losses. Generally speaking, if you think something was a loss, put it on your graph. <u>You can't really make a mistake in this exercise.</u>

## THIRD HOMEWORK ASSIGNMENT: PREPARING YOUR LOSS HISTORY GRAPH

With all of the preambles out of the way, it is time to begin. We will give you (both partners and those working alone) the instructions for the Loss History Graph exercise just as we do in our seminars.

1:  The entire exercise should not take you more than an hour. You may experience a wide range of emotional responses as the result of doing the Loss History Graph. Or you may have little or no emotional response. That is perfectly okay, do not be alarmed. Have a box of tissues handy. If you have an emotional reaction, let it be okay with you.

2:  The writing part of the exercise is nonverbal. It is best done alone and in silence.

3:  Get a pen or pencil and a piece of blank paper, at least the size of typing paper or standard notebook paper (8½" × 11"); legal-size paper (8½" × 14") is even better. Place the paper horizontally on your desk or table.

4:  Draw a straight line across the center of the page. Then divide your line into four equal parts, marking the sections lightly with a pencil. This will give you reference points for plotting dates.

Birthdate                    Mid Point                    Current Year

5: For example, if you are fifty years old, at the halfway point you were twenty-five. Write the year of your birth at the left end of the line. Write the current date on the right end of the line. Then plot your dawn of conscious memory, or earliest recollection, whether you perceive it as a loss or not, and mark it just after the year you were born.

6: Our examples began with our earliest conscious memory. If you think hard, you'll find that your first recollection will most likely fall between ages two and five, probably closer to five. It may be good or bad, happy or sad; it may be an event, an experience, an object, or a place. One of the easiest ways to establish an effective dawn-of-conscious-memory date is to remember something about your first house. Do not spend an inordinate amount of time establishing your dawn-of-conscious-memory date. It is merely a starting point.

7: You do not need to get the dates exactly right. We are much more interested in your emotional response to your losses.

8: Now take a few moments and ask yourself, "What is the most painful, life-limiting loss I have ever experienced?"

## TIME AND INTENSITY

All losses are experienced at **100** percent intensity when they occur. As we reflect, we recognize that some losses have had a greater impact on us than others. We have referred to the fact that relationships are composed of both time and intensity. Here is what we mean.

Russell had gone to the same dry cleaner, twice a week, for ten years. The same lady took his shirts and his money each time. He didn't know her name, so he referred to her as "the lady." One day when Russell went to pick up his shirts, a man came and took care of him. Russell said, "Where's the lady?" "Oh, she died." Russell felt a sense of sadness even though he had not known her name, nor anything about her. That relationship, although of many years' duration, had almost no intensity.

Russell was engaged to a young woman in 1964. This passionate relationship lasted only three months. When the romance crashed and burned, the two of them were not on good terms. He never spoke to her again. Thirty- two years

**later, Russell got a call from a mutual friend saying that she had died. This news had a powerful impact on him. The relationship, while short, had had tremendous emotional intensity.**

1: Identify your most painful loss. Find the approximate date point on your horizontal line and draw a vertical line downward to the bottom of the page. Make a notation of what the loss was: "Mom died," "Child died," "Divorce." You don't have to spend too much time writing out at length each separate grieving experience, as we did in our examples. Just make simple notes of words or phrases that will remind you of the loss.

2: After establishing and plotting your most painful loss experience, let your mind go back to your earliest memories and start marking down the loss events you remember. Use the length of the vertical line to establish the relative degree of intensity of the loss. Always make short notes so you will be able to recall what the loss was; for example, "Dog died," or, "Lost business."

Occasionally, you may realize that you have had both positive and negative responses to the same experiences. This is totally normal. For many people, their wedding day is simultaneously the most exciting of all days while also representing a "loss of freedom." The birth of a child can be exhilarating, on the one hand, and terrifying, on the other, as the parents take on new responsibilities. For the purposes of this exercise, however, we are focusing on the sad, negative, or painful aspects of these events. Grievers will often try to deal only with the positive side, so as to avoid the painful. That's one of the reasons you are using this book, so even if it seems uncomfortable, please stay with the loss perspective only.

If you find that a half-hour has gone by and all you have plotted is your dawn of conscious memory and one other loss, then take a break. Sometimes we try a little too hard and get stuck. Look back at John's and Russell's graphs. Their graphs will remind you of some of your losses.

It is not at all unnatural to sense some resistance in yourself. Remember, persistence will pay off in the long run. Our experience has shown us that most people over the age of fourteen have at least five losses to plot. For adults, the average is between ten and fifteen loss experiences.

Don't try to get this "right." Just be honest. There are no grades given for this work, and no one's approval is required. Abandon yourself to the exercise, and you will receive benefit directly proportional to the amount you put into it. But first, and now, you must begin!

## LEARNING FROM YOUR LOSS HISTORY GRAPH

Congratulations on finishing your graph!

The story of your life can be an eye-opening experience. It is imperative that you look at your losses to discover what misinformation you were taught directly or absorbed indirectly. It is equally essential that you not judge, evaluate, or criticize yourself for what you were shown or for interpretations you made.

Your first commitment in this regard is to be gentle with yourself about the discoveries you make. It can also be helpful to suspend judgment and criticism of those who taught you any incorrect ideas. Don't worry, you will have ample opportunity later to complete any thoughts and feelings about the sources of misinformation.

Having finished the graph, it is now time to examine it and see what you can learn. From your dawn of conscious memory onward, you may be able to get some very clear pictures about what you were influenced to believe. For those of you working with partners, you will soon see how many parallels there usually are between grieving people. In our seminars and outreach programs, people are often amazed at the losses and attitudes they have in common. While there are many parallels, we are still individuals. Scientists tell us that no two snowflakes, crystals, or grains of sand are alike, but they are made of the same ingredients. People are also unique. This exercise helps illustrate our human similarities and differences.

For those of you working alone, you might notice that some of your losses and attitudes are similar to some of John's and Russell's.

## FOURTH PARTNERS MEETING

Begin by reaffirming your commitments to total honesty, absolute confidentiality, and the uniqueness of your individual recovery. As always, meet in a private place where you will not feel uncomfortable if you cry. Have tissues handy.

*This meeting marks a change in how you will proceed.* These new guidelines will carry you through the balance of your meetings. Read them very carefully. Successful completion hinges on following these instructions.

Working with a partner does have benefits. One is the ability to verbalize what you have written. In order for this exercise to have the maximum value, we will give you some very strong guidelines, which we have developed over twenty years. We suggest that you adhere to them.

Make sure you bring your Loss History Graph and the two lists—on misinformation, and short-term energy-relieving behaviors—that you've already discussed.

**Instructions for the Listening Partner**

1. Sit a reasonable distance away. Avoid a sense of being in your partner's face or smothering him or her.
2. As the listening partner, you may laugh or cry, if appropriate, but *you may not talk!*
3. Do not touch your partner. Touch usually stops feelings.
4. Remember the image of being a heart with ears. Do your best to stay in the moment and really listen to your partner's story.

**Instructions for the Talking Partner**

1. Try to tell your loss history graph in half an hour or less. This is not a rigid rule, but be careful not to turn the entire meeting into a long monologue, which would have no value for you.
2. If you cry, try to keep talking while you cry. Push the words up and out, rather than swallowing them. People tend to choke off feelings in their throat.
3. When you finish your graph, ask your partner for a hug (assuming you've made hugs safe).
4. After getting your hug, take a few minutes to talk again about the misinformation you learned following your losses

as well as the short-term energy-relieving behaviors you may have participated in. This is an ideal opportunity to see the connection between your beliefs and the limits they may have put on your recovery.

Take a little break, and then let your partner do his or her graph.

Make plans for your next meeting.

## For Those Working Alone

Since you are working alone, you may find it effective to use John's and Russell's Loss History Graphs as your silent partner. Reread theirs, then look at yours. Notice the similarities and the differences. Once again, look at your STERBs. See if you notice any connection between your short-term relievers and your losses. Look at your lists of myths and beliefs to see whether they connect to the losses you have graphed.

# Part Three

## *Finding the Solution*

Welcome to the third part of this handbook. The solution is made up of five actions you must take in order to complete the pain caused by significant emotional loss. The actions that follow will require open-mindedness, much willingness, and courage. These actions and their meanings are:

1. Gaining awareness—that an incomplete emotional relationship exists.
2. Accepting responsibility—that in part you are the cause of the incompleteness.
3. Identifying recovery communications—that you have not delivered.
4. Taking actions—to communicate them.
5. Moving beyond loss—saying good-bye to undelivered communications and to pain.

# 10

# What Is Incompleteness?

Throughout this book we have referred to how we do things in our seminars. Most of the exercises translate easily into a format appropriate to a book, but some things require a little more explanation. One of them is coming to an understanding of exactly what constitutes emotional incompleteness.

In our three-day seminar for grievers, we are able to illustrate incompleteness by asking a few questions. On the second day, we ask one person whether he or she has had any positive thoughts or feelings about one of the other participants. When the answer is yes, we ask what the positive idea was. Usually it is something like, "I admired her courage," or, "I liked his openness." We ask, "Did you tell him?" The respondent says no. Then we ask, "What if he had died before you told him? Who would be left with the undelivered communication?" The response: "I would." Then we ask, "If you became incomplete with a stranger in one day, what have you done over a lifetime with family members, friends, and others?"

Incompleteness is not limited to major events. It is an accumulation of undelivered communications, large and small, that have emotional value to you. To the best of our knowledge, only the living grieve. It is essential that we complete what is unfinished for us.

Sometimes incompleteness is caused by our actions or non-actions. Other times it is caused by circumstances outside of our control.

One sad story illustrates unfinished emotions caused by circumstances.

A young boy ran across the front yard, hurrying to catch the school bus. As he ran, his mom yelled from the front porch, "Timmy, tuck in your shirt, what will the neighbors think?" Several hours later, the police knocked on the mother's front door. Her son Timmy had been killed in a freak accident in the schoolyard.

In addition to the unimaginable pain that the mother was suffering, which last communication do you think she wished had been different? We are not suggesting that if her last interaction with Timmy had been different, she would have felt any less pain. What we are suggesting is her last remark to her son definitely fits into the category of things we wish had ended *different, better, or more. We rarely ever know which interaction will be our last.* It is not abnormal in many of our relationships to table a few topics that we plan to deal with later. This is not necessarily procrastination, just a plan for later. But following a death or a divorce, such postponements often are some of the ingredients of incompleteness.

While death and divorce are obvious arenas for incomplete emotions, what about other losses? Often when we look back on difficult relationship with living people—parents, siblings, and others—we recognize many things that we wish had been *different, better, or more.* All too frequently, it is the accumulation of undelivered communications that limits us in these relationships as well.

Sometimes incompleteness is caused or exaggerated by others. Some people will not allow us to say meaningful things to them. Since we cannot force them to listen to us, we often get trapped with these undelivered communications, both positive and negative. Sometimes we are afraid to say emotionally charged things. Or we have been waiting for the right moment or circumstances. Sometimes the right time never comes. Or we forget. Or we get sidetracked. And then someone dies. And we are stuck with the undelivered emotional communication.

In short, emotional incompleteness is any undelivered emotional communication. Sometimes we're not sure what we said or did. This can cause feelings of incompleteness. Sometimes we are not sure whether the other person heard us, or whether they received our communication the way we intended. This also can leave us feeling unfinished.

*Please hear this.* Being emotionally incomplete does not mean that you are bad. It does not mean that you are defective. It only means that a variety of circumstances and actions or nonactions have robbed you of the opportunity to be complete.

## HOW TO IDENTIFY WHAT IS INCOMPLETE

In essence, your Loss History Graph was an itemization of past grieving experiences. At the end of this section are instructions for using your Loss History Graph to help identify which loss or losses are still emotionally incomplete. As you look at your Loss History Graph, you may sense a wide range of emotions attached to the people, the events, and the relationships listed there. When reminded of a loss, you might feel sad. This is entirely normal.

Your objective is to discover those relationships that are incomplete. In order to do so, it is helpful if you can try to distinguish between pain and sadness. Some of the clues that might help you are:

1. If you are unwilling to think about or talk about someone who has died, or any other loss, that may signify unresolved grief.
2. If fond memories turn painful, you may be experiencing unresolved grief.
3. If you want to talk only about positive aspects of the relationship, it might be unresolved grief.
4. Wanting to talk only about negative aspects of the relationship may be a sign of unresolved grief.
5. Unresolved grief may be at the root of any fear associated with thoughts or feelings about the relationship.

We have feelings in response to every life change that occurs. Most of these changes are small and insignificant and cause little or no discomfort. Yet some have had a lasting impact on our attitudes and outlooks on life. The more intense these feelings are, the higher the probability that they are unresolved or incomplete.

Motivation to attend our seminars and outreach programs is usually prompted by a recent loss. The actions of recovery usually lead to an awareness that you have other incomplete relationships. You may make a similar discovery as you work through this book.

## CHOOSING A LOSS TO COMPLETE

You are ready to identify the loss that is most incomplete for you. While it could be a death, remember, loss is not limited to death. For most people, divorce implies emotional incompleteness. Many of our relationships with living people—parents, siblings, other relatives, friends—may also be incomplete.

**Instructions**

1. Get out your Loss History Graph. Circle the losses with which you think you might still be incomplete. Be honest in your assessment. It doesn't matter how many losses you list or how long ago they happened. If you don't know whether you're incomplete with respect to a loss on your graph, circle it.

2. Use the idea of time and/or intensity coupled with your own honest sense of what is unfinished or what is still painful for you. Be realistic here. If your infant died, the relationship may not have had much time but will certainly have had tremendous intensity. Therefore, the death of your child might be the correct first choice for you.

3. There is a strong possibility that the loss that brought you to this book may not be the one you wind up working on first. If that occurs, let it be okay. However, we don't want you to choose a less intense loss out of fear or avoidance of a more painful one.

4. The loss that is most incomplete for you may not appear on your Loss History Graph. Be alert to the fact that your most incomplete relationship might be with a living person who does not appear as a "loss."

5. Don't spend more than an hour in this process of elimination. You will confuse yourself. The real question is simply,

"Which of the losses in my life is limiting and restricting me the most right now?"

6. Choose one. You cannot make a major error in choosing which relationship to work on. If there are several incomplete relationships in your life, you will eventually work on them all. *Note: You cannot do your parents together. You must do each relationship, one at a time.* For now, we want you to choose the relationship that seems to embody the most pain or the most unfinished emotion, or both.

## MORE HELP CHOOSING THE FIRST LOSS TO WORK ON AND QUESTIONS ABOUT OTHER LOSSES

Over the years people have asked us which loss to work on first. A common question comes from people who had a parent die when they were young—usually between birth and age 10. Although that death dramatically affected their lives, they wonder if it's the correct first loss to work on.

We also get inquiries about losses other than death and divorce. Those questions often involve alcoholism, mental illness, and various kinds of abuse; or about dealing with Alzheimer's and similar conditions. And many people ask us how to deal with loss of faith, or career or health issues.

A new section called *More on Choices and Other Losses* begins on page 167. It contains additional explanations about choosing the first loss to work on, and guidance for dealing with "other losses." Even if you've already chosen which loss to work on first, we suggest you read the new section before you start the Relationship Graph exercise in the next chapter.

# 11

# Introducing the Relationship Graph

To create an accurate memory picture of a relationship, it is helpful to use a clear-cut format. Over the years we have developed an extremely simple process that is very likely to help you discover what is unfinished for you.

As always, we recommend that you not take shortcuts. If you use the format exactly as suggested, it is almost always successful. In fact, most problems occur when someone tries to change the format.

## THE RELATIONSHIP GRAPH IS DIFFERENT FROM THE LOSS HISTORY GRAPH

In the Loss History Graph, we focused on loss; we listed sad, painful, or negative life events that we remembered. The point of the Relationship Graph is to take a complete and detailed look at one relationship. Positive or happy events are marked above the center line, and negative or sad events below the line.

At some point after a loss occurs, our brains begin a review, searching for what was never communicated or completed. You may or may not be aware that this review began very soon after the loss. In fact, the review continues intermittently until the loss is completed. The purpose of the Relationship Graph is to help you tap into that review and use it to discover what is unfinished for you so that you can then complete it.

## COMPLETING IS NOT FORGETTING

To resolve an emotionally incomplete loss, you must complete it. Completing does not mean that you will forget your loved one. What we are completing is our relationship to the pain caused by the loss. We are completing anything that was left unfinished at the time of the loss. The only thing that can stop you now is the fear that you'll forget your loved one. *That is not possible.*

The three aspects of relationships that we focus on are physical, emotional, and spiritual.

Death ends the physical relationship we had. We can no longer touch or speak to the other person in the same way. Divorce dramatically changes the physical relationship we had with our spouse. We do not touch them or even talk with them in the same way.

Emotional relationships include all of the feelings we may have about another person or even a pet. Those feelings are not limited to happy or positive but include painful and negative emotions. When a death or divorce occurs, we must discover and complete whatever is incomplete at the time of the loss. While the physical relationship ended or changed, the emotional relationship continues in our memory.

The spiritual aspect of our relationships is more difficult to define. We all have differing ideas about spirituality. For our purposes, spiritual aspects are those that are neither physical nor emotional. It is that intangible something that makes you sense a connection to others. Your spiritual connection also does not end when a death or divorce occurs.

Since grief is the normal and natural emotional response to loss, the vast majority of this book relates to emotions. Successful completion of unfinished emotions allows us to become complete with the often painful reality that the physical relationship has ended.

Grief recovery affects the quality of your life. Completion of unfinished emotions does not interfere with any religious, philosophical, or spiritual beliefs you may have about seeing someone again in heaven.

## ACCURATE MEMORY PICTURES: YOUR PART

We talked about grievers having a tendency to create larger-than-life memory pictures. It is unlikely that you would be able to complete with someone you consider a saint or a devil. You can complete your loss only by acknowledging the truth. If you recall, the first commitment you made in this book was to tell the truth. Enshrinement or bedevilment is *not the truth.*

We've talked to grievers following the death of a loved one, and in no time at all they began telling us about someone who never made a mistake in his or her entire life. They talk only about the good and positive aspects of their loved one. When we listen closely, we'll even hear: "I should have appreciated him more while I had him. He was a perfect husband." We have heard the same kind of comments following the breakup of long-term romantic relationships and marriages. *This kind of exaggerated, one-sided memory is really the function of a broken heart that does not know a better way to communicate the truth.*

As much as you love the person who died, or even the person you are divorced from, he or she was not perfect—as you are not perfect. Every relationship, even the most ideal, has its ups and downs. When you are taking these grief recovery actions, you can only be responsible for your part. If you're remembering your loved ones as you wish they were, not as they truly were, it becomes impossible to complete your emotional relationship with them. An accurate memory of your loved ones is much stronger and will be cherished more than a fantasy about them.

## TRUTH IS THE KEY TO RECOVERY

The essence of recovery is contained in the premise of being totally honest about *ourselves* in relation to others. However, as humans, it is virtually impossible not to have impressions and opinions about others. So we must allow that our perception of others may limit or restrict our recovery. Being supercritical of what others did or did not do usually leads to an inaccurate appraisal of our relationship with them.

It may seem that this book is overly directed at helping people complete their relationship with a "loved one" who has died. We're sure there are many people reading this book who still grieve about someone they didn't like. Your feelings may be ones of strong resentment or even hate. Even so, this program of grief recovery will work for you. We will have more to say about resentments in relationships as we progress through the recovery actions.

We are going to take an in-depth look at a relationship with an eye to discovering what we wish had ended *different, better, or more*, as well as the unrealized hopes, dreams, and expectations about the future. We will be looking for the things we wish we had said or not said. We will be looking for the things we wish we had done or not done. And we will be looking for the things we wish the other person had said or done.

Some relationships are more loving than others. Indeed, some relationships are more complete than others. However, we have yet to meet anyone who had no undelivered emotional communications at all. We have met people who were afraid or unwilling to look honestly at their own part of what might have been unfinished. We have met people who had so much misinformation as to believe that anything honest they might say could hurt someone who had died.

Let us reemphasize at this point that the motive is not to hurt or destroy memories or relationships. This remains a private acknowledgment, confined to yourself or to a partner who is sworn to confidentiality.

## EVEN LONG ILLNESSES END IN UNFINISHED BUSINESS

Question: After a long-term illness, during which you took care of your dying loved one twenty-four hours a day and talked with him or her about everything, could there still be something unfinished between you? Answer: *Yes!*

Why? Partially because both the patient and the caretaker are preoccupied during a long-term illness with treatment, comfort, and medication. Partially because it is virtually impossible to talk directly with someone exactly as you would talk to someone else about him or her. And finally, because the death itself provokes an intensity of review that cannot be duplicated while the loved one is still alive. Let us illustrate that point. If you have been involved in a loved one's long-term illness, you will recall that no matter how well you may have thought you were prepared, no matter how willing you were to accept what was going to happen, you were still massively affected when the death actually happened. The finality, the absoluteness, of death upgrades what the brain can do in its search for unfinished business.

Is divorce the same? Yes and no. Divorce is the death of a relationship as well as the accompanying hopes, dreams, and expectations. Feelings about the end of a relationship can begin long before any legal proceedings are initiated. For some, the feelings start during the trip to a lawyer to start a divorce. For others, the feelings don't click in until the formal declaration of divorce is issued by the state. When the sense of finality kicks in, it unleashes the same powerful search by the brain and the heart for things unfinished. But while death automatically signals the *end* of the physical relationship, divorce *changes* the physical relationship.

## HOPES, DREAMS, AND EXPECTATIONS

**Death is never a singular event. In addition to the actual death, there is the death of all the hopes, dreams, and expectations about the future. Divorces and other relationship breakups conform to the same idea.**

In positive relationships, our hopes and dreams relate to the ongoing experience of being together and all the events that are likely to occur over time. Many couples look forward to retirement. They have extensive plans for traveling and pursuing a whole host of hobbies and recreations. All too often, one partner dies before the couple is able to actualize all of those plans. Many of our other positive relationships contain visions for the future. Those pictures also end with a death.

In negative relationships, there is inevitably the hope that someday we will get some fences mended, or that the other person will apologize for what we believe he or she has done to harm us. Many people grew up in dysfunctional homes, surrounded by alcoholism or other debilitating conditions. As children, they didn't always know there was a different way to live. Sometimes, as adults, they realize that they missed out on a normal, healthy childhood. It is essential that they grieve and complete the pain from their childhood. In effect, they must look backward at what they now realize would have been normal hopes, dreams, and expectations.

Some people have horrible relationships with parents or siblings. Occasionally, they are able to work out their differences and arrive at a new positive relationship. As they reunite, they automatically begin to have normal hopes, dreams, and expectations about the future. Much too often, these rekindled relationships are cut short by an untimely death. "I finally got my dad back. We had so much catching up to do. But he had a sudden heart attack and died before we could really begin to enjoy each other."

It is essential that you understand the power of the unfinished emotions attached to future events. You will see and hear many things that remind you of the plans you had with the one who died, or from whom you are divorced. It is important to complete as much as you can now, to help you in the future when there are other reminders.

## THE RELATIONSHIP GRAPH

Soon we will give you instructions for making your relationship graph. We will start by giving you examples.

### John's Relationship Graph with His Younger Brother

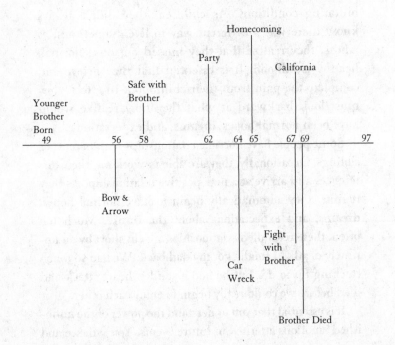

*'49—My younger brother is born.* It isn't marked above or below the line. That's because I want to tell you a story of poor communication. I'm sure I noticed my mother was pregnant, and I must have asked her what it meant. When she told me it meant I'd have a new brother or sister, I was happy. But I must have been confused because I thought he'd be my size when he arrived. I already had an older brother, so I knew brothers were my size. When they brought him home, I was shocked. He wasn't even big enough to play ball with us. That's my first conscious memory of my younger brother.

*'56—My younger brother breaks my bow and arrow.* I was angry about it. I'd told him to leave it alone, but he was only seven and wanted to do all the things his older brothers did. I was pretty rough on him and made him cry.

*'58—My brother comes to me for comfort and protection.* Our parents had been arguing, and he was terrified. He came and crawled into my bed and wanted to know if he could stay with me. I felt very proud that he knew he was safe with me.

*'62—I go into the military service.* My older brother and younger brother had a going-away party for me. They both told me they loved me and to be safe. I always knew they loved me, but it was nice to hear.

*'64—My younger brother wrecks my car.* I was overseas and had told him not to use my car. Fifteen-year-olds don't listen well. So one day, when my mother was at work, he decided to go for a ride. The ride ended up a telephone pole.

*'65—I come home from the service.* When my brother opened the front door, I couldn't believe he had grown so much. He had grown taller than me. He'd become the man of the house. I was proud of him.

*'67—My younger brother lives with me in California.* If you'll notice, the graph is marked both above and below the line.

We had our ups and downs. He didn't want to come home when I wanted him to. I got to see what it was like to be a parent. He wouldn't make his bed, wouldn't put gas in the car, ran up huge phone bills calling his girlfriend back home. At the same time, we went places together, laughed, and had a great time. He and I became friends as well as brothers.

This was also the year of our biggest argument. He was talking about getting married. I didn't think that was a very good idea. We fought like cats and dogs. He eventually stayed in school and the situation calmed down. I never took the time to clear up the bad feelings.

*'69—My brother dies.* Our last conversation was over the phone. He and his friends were on their way to visit me in California. They'd stopped for the day and decided to nap. Before doing that, he called me on the phone. The boys were in Las Vegas. They'd never been there before and wanted to see the lights. As usual, he was out of money and wanted to "borrow" some. I told him to go to one of the hotels where I had some friends and they'd give him some money. I hung up after saying, "See you tomorrow."

I never saw him tomorrow. He died that afternoon. How I wished, at the time, that my last conversation had included "I love you." There were other times I wished our conversations had been more feeling-oriented and honest.

John knew and loved his brother for twenty years, but when he did the Relationship Graph for the first time, not many events came to light. When he did start to remember events, at first glance they seemed trivial. Nevertheless, they were associated with the feelings he wished he had acknowledged. It was these undelivered communications he wished had been *different, better, or more.*

We turn now to Russell's Relationship Graph, where the undelivered communications are highlighted in bold.

## Russell's Relationship Graph with His Former Wife Vivienne

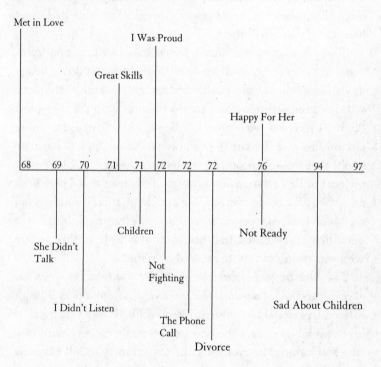

'68—*We meet on a Sunday.* Her name was Vivienne. We married on Tuesday. For me, she was The One. I was smitten. She was very cute. Being from London, she was sophisticated. Looking back, I realize that while she was only nineteen, her English accent and London ways made her seem older to me. I was twenty-five.

*'69—Sometimes she appears to be upset with me.* My complaint was not that she was upset with me, but how she did or didn't communicate about it. She was always very quiet, but even more so when there was a problem. **I had to forgive her for her unwillingness and inability to tell me what was going on.** I often felt in the dark, and I resorted to guessing what had upset her. It was very frustrating.

*'70—I have strong opinions about how we should run our business.* I am very verbal and can be self-righteous and dominating. Try as she might, she could not get me to budge off some self-defeating attitudes. She tried to reason with me, but most often I overruled her. Many of the decisions I made in those circumstances led to real business problems later. I have no doubt that they also contributed to our divorce. As I looked at my part of that relationship honestly, I realized that I owed her an apology for being overbearing and dogmatic. Not only was I sorry for what happened to me and the business, **but I was genuinely sorry that I had not been able to hear this person who was trying to talk to me and help me.**

*'71—Our unique abilities create a nice combination when we open our restaurant together.* We were very different people, with different personalities and different skills. I was the friendly host and kibitzer, and she was exceptionally creative with cuisine and baking. **I never took the opportunity to tell her how much I appreciated her skills and the wonderful balance she brought to the business aspect of our lives.**

*'71—She wants to have children.* Personality issues aside, we did not have too many major differences of opinions or philosophies. We were mostly in agreement about what we were doing and where we hoped it would lead—except in one major area. Vivienne wanted children. It seemed very important to her. Having struggled so much of my early life, and

finally feeling some freedom, I was not at all ready to have children. **I had to forgive her for any part the issue of children played in her request for a divorce. I also needed to apologize for not knowing and telling the truth about myself sooner.**

During our whirlwind four years together, there was tremendous joy. We entertained and were entertained by celebrities. We were the "toast of the town." It was exciting to be with her at events. Being caught in the energy of our lifestyle and our business, I did not always remember to stop and tell her about the important emotions I was experiencing. While we said the obligatory "I love you" every night, **I didn't tell her how much she meant to me, how proud I was to be seen with her, and how wonderful I thought she was.**

I was usually preoccupied with the daily goings-on in our restaurant. I was not as conscious of what was going on in our marriage. *I have already said that I owed her an apology for my overbearing ways.* It would be unrealistic to look at this relationship and conclude that it was only my part or my flaws that destroyed it. While I needed to apologize for my self-righteous verbal dominance, **I also had to forgive her for her quietness and unwillingness to fight for what she believed in—for giving up and giving in.**

*'72—She initiates a divorce.* As the marriage progressed, there was great confusion for me. On the one hand, I was blissfully happy and unaware that there was trouble in paradise. We had a successful business and, to the best of my limited awareness, a happy marriage. On the other hand, those problem areas, which I can now see with great clarity, were building up a head of steam. One day my wife called me and announced that she was leaving me and applying for a divorce. That telephone call sticks out in my memory. She did not try to talk to me in person, she did it on the phone. **For**

**me, it was another example of how poorly she communi-
cated, and I needed to forgive her for doing it that way.**

For me, the divorce was very sudden. In the first several
weeks following the divorce, I must have walked and talked,
but I remember almost nothing. My only conscious awareness
about loss was to *be strong for others.* Now I was the "other," and
I did not know what to do. During that time, I had a revelation.
It dawned on me that my greatest complaint in the relationship
was her unwillingness to talk when there was a problem. On
the other hand, I realized that when she did talk, I did not listen. I did not know what to do with this awareness. **It was to be
much later before I learned that I needed to forgive her for not
talking and apologize to her for not listening.**

The divorce ended the marital relationship. While divorce
ends most of the physical aspects of the relationship, the emotional and spiritual aspects continue. In divorce, the emotional
and spiritual components often change more radically than they
do following a death. In the more than twenty-five years since
my divorce from Vivienne, a few notable events have helped me
discover some additional incompleteness in my relationship
with her.

*'76—Vivienne tells me that she and her new husband have ad-
opted two baby boys.* Shortly thereafter, she became pregnant
and delivered a baby girl. My reaction at the time was very
mixed. Of course, I was thrilled for her. I had always believed
she would be a fabulous mother. But a part of me was hurt. I
recalled some old hopes, dreams, and expectations that I had
held when she and I were together. **I needed to forgive her for
not waiting for me to be ready for children.**

(There is one last important emotional detail about my relationship to Vivienne. In 1974 I met and married Jeanne. When
Jeanne and I got together, her daughter Kelly was five years

old. I have been Kelly's dad for a long time now. As such, I have been able to have all of the feelings associated with being a parent. Kelly is a total joy to me, and I treasure our relationship.)

*'94—A dear friend of mine adopts a baby girl and names her Gabrielle.* She quickly became Gabi, and even more quickly captured my heart. She was seven months old when she came into my life. I immediately nominated myself as number-one uncle. I even had a baby seat installed in my car. From her very first days here, she had me wrapped around her little, little finger. At first, my girlfriend Alice and I were a little baffled at the attention I was paying to this baby.

One day, while delivering a Grief Recovery Seminar, I started talking about Gabi. The next thing I knew, there were tears in my eyes. I realized what was going on. Kelly had been five years old when she came into my life. I had never had the experience of interacting with an infant. Although I was just the "uncle," I did many things with Gabi. I taught her how to crawl, ride ponies, play jacks, and throw a baseball.

As that revelation sank in, I was struck with a deep awareness of what I had missed with Vivienne. I had not had the chance to be a parent with her. I was saddened. Since I had already made my indirect apologies and forgiven her, what was left was the picture of us as parents that I had held in my heart since first meeting her in 1968. **How sad I was that we had not had children together.**

## FOURTH HOMEWORK ASSIGNMENT: MAKING YOUR RELATIONSHIP GRAPH

To start your Relationship Graph, both those working as partners and those working alone must have chosen one relationship to work on first. Use a sheet of paper at least 8½" × 11". Turn the paper sideways and draw a line from left to right across the middle of the page. The left end of the line represents the beginning of the relationship. If you are graphing a parent, that date is probably the same as your dawn of conscious memory. For all other relationships, it is the year you met the person. The right end of the line represents the current year; enter it now. If you are graphing a death or divorce, mark the year of that event in the appropriate place. Relationships do not end with death or divorce.

## DAWN OF MEMORY—
## THE DEATH OF AN INFANT

If you are dealing with grief caused by the death of a child (stillborn birth, miscarriage, abortion, or sudden infant death syndrome [SIDS]), the dawn-of-conscious-memory event will start a bit earlier than it does in most other relationships. Generally speaking, when a woman realizes she is pregnant, *her emotional relationship with her child begins.* Women also describe a change in their feelings when they feel the first flutter inside their body. For the next few weeks, she is constantly saying to her husband, "Can't you feel the movement?" The husband dutifully puts his hand on her tummy but can't feel anything yet. He finally feels the small kick, and *that's when his emotional relationship begins.* It's an imaginary physical relationship at this point, but it's emotionally real. When John's wife became pregnant with his son (the one who died in 1977) and he felt the first movement, his mind immediately began to create hopes, dreams, and expectations. His child was going to have all the things that he didn't have when he was growing up. Although there was no physical relationship yet, it was emotionally real for both John and his wife.

Throughout this book, we have talked about completing a relationship that actually existed, but with the death of an infant, we need to complete a relationship that was supposed to be but never was. When John's son died, he can remember standing outside the nursery and thinking, "He'll never know all the things I was going to do for him. He's never going to know how much I loved him." These were the hopes and dreams he had that would not be realized because of the death. All parents want to give their children all the things they didn't have while growing up. Once this idea is set, what do you do with the thoughts and feelings if the child doesn't live? This type of problem needs to be completed as much as any other.

Next, go to the beginning and reconstruct the relationship to the best of your ability. Your goal is to identify undelivered communications. Let your memory wander. Mark down whatever pops into your mind. Decide whether events are positive (above the line) or negative (below the line). Your mind may or may not go in chronological order. Identify misunderstandings as well as memorable events. Don't edit or limit. Just recall and note. Honesty and thoroughness are essential. Look back at Russell's comments about the incidents on his graph and the undelivered emotional communications associated with each one.

*Do not judge what happened.* Don't fall into the trap of trying to intellectualize. We're looking for the feelings you had when these events happened. Keep the graph centered on the relationship. Otherwise, it can shift in focus to other surrounding relationships.

Our suggestion is to set aside about an hour and then start. Try to remember at least ten events to plot. If you get stuck, look back at the examples in the book. They may trigger your own memories.

To maintain truth and accuracy and avoid enshrinement or bedevilment, we recommend that you have at least two events above the line and at least two events below the line. Some of you may find it difficult to allow yourself to remember anything negative about a positive relationship. On the other hand, some of you will struggle to identify positive events in your relationship with a less than loved one. For instance, in our memories of an abusive parent, we typically find it difficult to remember positive aspects of the relationship or to assign a positive value to anything about it. To avoid the danger of an inaccurate, larger-than-life picture, we must take pains to be honest. While a parent may have been abusive at many levels, he or she may also have paid the rent and provided food and clothing. Remembering the positive contributions of an abusive parent is not done to minimize the bad things he or she did, but to allow us to arrive at a truthful portrayal of the relationship. All relationships are made up of good and bad, right and wrong, sweet and sour.

Some relationships are mixed and over time may go from good to bad and back. It is very typical to have a good early relationship with a parent, then some rocky teenage years, followed by an excellent adult relationship. You must review the whole relationship. You probably will discover some aspects of incidents during the rocky periods that were not communicated. Do not think that since your recent relationship was good, all previous problems and incidents had been completed.

You get to be the judge. Do not be influenced by what others might think. A woman in one of our seminars listed as one of her fondest memories the times her daddy took her into a saloon and sat her up on the bar while he drank and joked with his buddies. Others might comment that it was abusive to take a little girl into that environment. Others don't get a vote in your memories of your relationship. All that matters is what is accurate for you.

Positive memories can range from sitting together on the porch to going on vacation, holding hands as the sun set, or raising children together. A new dress or toy, swimming lessons, or coaching from a parent might be remembered with tremendous fondness. Do not dismiss a memory because you think it too small. The accumulation of small undelivered communications contributes to incomplete relationships.

An unhappy or negative memory can be as simple as a disagreement. As a child, punishments are often remembered with great intensity. Especially important are those punishments for infractions you did not commit. The unfairness associated with a false punishment often carries lifelong weight. As with the positive memories, no negative memories are too small or insignificant for this exercise.

Use the length of your lines, above and below the horizontal, to indicate the intensity of your feelings at the time the event occurred. It doesn't matter whether there are more events above or below the line; it only matters that what's on the graph is the truth. Don't be concerned with what others will think or say—no one else will see this graph.

Now it's your turn. Begin.

## FIFTH PARTNERS MEETING

Congratulations on finishing your Relationship Graph! In this meeting, the partners will share those graphs. Begin by reaffirming your commitments to total honesty, absolute confidentiality, and the uniqueness of your individual recovery. As always, meet in a private place where you will not feel uncomfortable if you cry. Have tissues handy.

Make sure you bring your Relationship Graphs.

### Instructions for the Listening Partner
1. Sit a reasonable distance away. Avoid being in your partner's face or smothering him or her.
2. You may laugh or cry, if appropriate, but *you may not talk!*
3. Do not touch your partner. Touch usually stops feelings.
4. Remember the image of being a heart with ears. Do your best to stay in the moment and really listen to your partner's story.

### Instructions for the Talking Partner
1. Start by telling the story of the relationship you have graphed, beginning either at your dawn of conscious memory or at the date when you first met the person. Generally, a graph about a parent begins at the dawn of conscious memory, while a graph about a spouse begins in the year you met. Here is an example of each: "I was born in 1943, but my first conscious awareness of my father was in 1947, when I was four years old. I remember him taking me for a milkshake. I had strawberry, and it is still my favorite flavor." "I first met my wife at a friend's party. I'll never forget the feeling of my breath being taken away as I thought how beautiful she was."

2. As you move through the events on your graph, you will in-tuitively fill in many aspects of the story of your relationship with that person. Be careful not to go off on tangents, espe-cially about other relationships. Also be careful not to turn your story into a monologue. Telling your relationship story should take about half an hour. It's okay to go a little over, but not much. It's most effective to stick to the events you have graphed.

3. If you cry, try to talk while you cry. Push the words up and out, rather than swallowing them. We all tend to choke off feelings in our throats.

4. When you finish telling the story, get a hug from your part-ner (assuming you've made hugs safe). Both of you should avoid the trap of discussing what you have just done. This is when you run the risk of creating a sense of judgment, eval-uation, or criticism.

Take a little break, and then let your partner do his or her graph.

Make your plans for your next meeting.

## For Those Working Alone

Since you are working alone, you may find it effective to use John's and Russell's Relationship Graphs as your silent partner. Reread theirs, then look at yours. Notice the similarities and the differences.

# 12

# Almost Home:
# Converting the Relationship Graph
# into Recovery Components

To communicate and complete the discoveries made in your Relationship Graph, you must first put them into one of the following three categories.

Apologies
Forgiveness
Significant emotional statements

As simple as they may seem, these three categories are sufficient to convey any undelivered emotional communication.

## APOLOGIES

You make apologies for anything *you did or did not do* that might have hurt someone else. You may owe an apology for something you actually did ("I'm sorry for taking the money from your purse") or for something you did not do ("I'm sorry I didn't visit you in the hospital"). Or you may not have communicated something positive before the death or divorce ("I'm sorry for not thanking you for the present"). In this category, we are primarily concerned with you and your perception of your own actions or nonactions. If you have any sense that something you did or did not do might have harmed or offended the other person, then put it down. It is important to avoid judging yourself. The objective is to become complete, not to hurt yourself further. For the most part, your apologies are a private communication between you and your partner. Occasionally, you will discover an apology that can safely be made to a living person. Some apologies, however, should and must remain indirect.

## VICTIMS HAVE DIFFICULTY WITH APOLOGIES

Some people develop lifelong relationships with their pain and act like victims. This often becomes a life-limiting and restricting habit. Most people who do this are not aware that it has become an almost automatic reaction to most life circumstances.

It is horrible that anyone is ever mistreated. It is obviously appalling when children, who have no effective means of defending themselves, are mistreated.

"Victims" have a hard time apologizing. The memorized sense of victimhood often creates inaccurate pictures. Nevertheless, there is a need to apologize for your transgressions, no matter how slight, no matter how infrequent. Remember, you cannot be complete with anything less than the whole truth.

*Sometimes our desire to be right can be a big problem in making apologies.* Our sense of rightness or self-righteousness keeps us from being totally honest about our actions and nonactions. Be especially alert to this possibility if you are working on your relationship with a less than loved one. There is a tendency to get caught up in the idea that the other person has harmed you. While true, that does not eliminate your need to make apologies for what you have done to them.

## FORGIVENESS

Forgiveness is *giving up the hope of a different or better yesterday.*

Forgiveness is one of the least understood concepts in the world. Most people seem to convert the word *forgive* into the word *condone.* The definitions in *Merriam-Webster's Tenth Collegiate Dictionary* illustrate the problem:

FORGIVE: "to cease to feel resentment against (an offender)."

CONDONE: "to treat as if trivial, harmless, or of no importance."

If we believe the two words to be synonymous, it would be virtually impossible to forgive. The implication that we might trivialize a horrible event is clearly unacceptable. However, if we use *Webster's* definition of *forgive,* we are on the right track.

Any memorized resentment of past events will limit and restrict our ability to participate fully in life. Any reminder of the person or event may stimulate a painful reliving of the unfinished emotions attached to it. Successful recovery requires completion of the pain rather than retention of the resentment.

The subject of forgiveness carries with it many beliefs passed on from generation to generation. Some people have developed such a massive resistance to the word *forgive* that they cannot use it. We recently helped such a woman. She called it the "F" word. We gave her the following phrase: *I acknowledge the things that you did or did not do that hurt me, and I am not going to let them hurt me anymore.* A variation is: *I acknowledge the things that you did or did not do that hurt me, and I'm not going to let my memory of those incidents hurt me anymore.*

The insensitive, unconscious, and sometimes evil actions of other people have hurt us. Our continued resentment and inability to forgive hurts us, not them. Imagine that the perpetrator has died. Can your continued resentment harm him or her? Clearly not! Can it harm you? Unfortunately, yes. As with all recovery components, the objective of our actions is to set us free. We forgive in order to reacquire our own sense of well-being. *Forgiveness has nothing to do with the other person.*

## Forgiveness Is an Action, Not a Feeling

You cannot feel forgiveness until you do it. Many people say, "I can't forgive him, I don't feel it." To which we say: Of course not. You cannot feel something you have not done. A feeling of forgiveness can result only from the action of verbalizing the forgiveness. Action first, feeling follows.

Forgiveness is giving up the resentment you hold against another person. You may need to forgive them for something they actually did ("I forgive you for ruining my birthday party") or for something they did not do ("I forgive you for not attending my graduation").

There is a strange expression: "I can forgive, but I can't

forget." It mixes two separate ideas that are not directly connected. Imagine that you were horribly beaten over many years. It is not even vaguely possible to forget those incidents. The implication of "I can forgive, but I can't forget" is that, since I cannot forget, I will not forgive. But ask yourself: Who stays in jail? Who continues to resent and shut down his or her own mind, body, and heart? Whose life is limited by the lack of forgiveness?

We are often asked whether, in dealing with living people, it is appropriate to forgive someone in person. Our response is: *NO! NO! NO!* An unsolicited statement of forgiveness is almost always perceived as an attack. The person being forgiven need never know that it has happened. *Remember, never forgive anyone directly to their face.*

One last note: many people ask others to forgive them. We think this is a very incorrect communication. In fact, when you ask for forgiveness, you are manipulating: you are asking the other person to do something that you need to do. And when you ask someone who has died to forgive you, you are asking a dead person to take an action. Spiritual beliefs aside, it is clear that *you need to take an action*, not ask someone else to do it for you. If you are asking for forgiveness, you are really trying to apologize for something you have said or done. Don't try. Do it. Don't ask for forgiveness. Make an apology.

## SIGNIFICANT EMOTIONAL STATEMENTS

Any undelivered emotional communication that is neither an apology nor a forgiveness conveniently falls into the catchall category of significant emotional statemens. Here is a list of examples:

I loved you.
I hated you.
I was very proud of you.
I was very ashamed of you.
Thank you for the sacrifices you made for me.
I appreciated the time you spent with me.

This category is both simple and profound. It allows you to convey any and all undelivered communications that have been keeping you incomplete. Although any one statement may appear to be minor, *it is the accumulation of a lifetime of unsaid things that contributes to a sense of incompleteness.*

We have used the phrase *different, better, or more* many times throughout this book. Here is an explanation of that phrase: Following a death or divorce, we almost always discover some things that we wish we had said or done, or some things that we wish that we hadn't said or done. We also remember things we wish the other person had or hadn't said or done. These are some of the undelivered communications that fall into the category, *significant emotional statements.* When relationships end or change through death, divorce, or other circumstances, we almost always have a sense of broken *hopes, dreams, and expectations.* Attached to our awareness of them are significant emotional statements. Now is the time to put words on the thoughts and feelings that the loss robbed us of the opportunity to communicate.

In dealing with living people, it is never appropriate to make a negative significant emotional statement to them. Any negative comment will be perceived as an attack.

Congratulations on finishing your Relationship Graph.

## FIFTH HOMEWORK ASSIGNMENT:
## PUTTING IT ALL TOGETHER

It is now time to translate your Relationship Graph into the recovery components: apologies, forgiveness, and significant emotional statements. Take a fresh sheet of paper and set it up as follows:

Apologies:

Forgiveness:

Significant Emotional Statements:

Now take out your Relationship Graph. Go through it one event at a time and assign a recovery category to each event. Generally, above-the-line events will be either apologies or significant emotional statements. Below-the-line events will be either forgiveness or significant emotional statements. Some events will require two categories, especially negative events. For example: "Dad, thank you for taking me to my ball game" (significant emotional statement). But, "I need to forgive you for telling me that I was the worst player there" (forgiveness).

Many events on your graph will have a corresponding entry in at least one recovery category. Don't be overly concerned if you repeat communications that you think you may have already said to someone. Don't worry if there's more than one event with the same recovery communication. Later you will have an opportunity to refine everything you have done in this exercise. Don't edit. Just get it all down on paper.

## SIXTH PARTNERS MEETING

In this meeting, you will share your lists of recovery communications. Begin by reaffirming your commitments to total honesty, absolute confidentiality, and to the uniqueness of your individual recovery. As always, meet in a private place where you will not feel uncomfortable if you cry. Have tissues handy.

Make sure you bring your Relationship Graph and your three lists of recovery categories (apologies, forgiveness, and significant emotional statements).

### Instructions for the Listening Partner
1. Sit a reasonable distance away. Avoid being in your partner's face or smothering him or her.
2. You may laugh or cry, if appropriate, but *you may not talk!*
3. Do not touch your partner. Touch usually stops feelings.
4. Remember the image of being a heart with ears. Do your best to stay in the moment and really listen to your partner's story.

### Instructions for the Talking Partner
1. It is time for you to read your list of apologies, forgiveness, and significant emotional statements. There is no perfect way to do this, but here is one method that works for most.

Start with the apologies category: "I need to apologize to my father for the times I took money out of his pocket." Or, "I owe my mother an apology for lying to her about staying out late." In this exercise, we are acknowledging the need to make these recovery communications. We will actually make them in our next assignment.

2. Use the same technique with the forgiveness category: "I need to forgive my dad," and so on. Do the same for significant emotional statements: "I need to tell Dad how much . . . ," and so on.

3. If you cry, try to talk while you cry. Push the words up and out, rather than swallowing them. We all tend to choke off feelings in our throats.

4. When you finish your lists, get a hug from your partner (assuming you've made hugs safe). Both of you should avoid the trap of discussing what you have just done. This is when you run the risk of creating a sense of judgment, evaluation, or criticism and of overintellectualizing.

Take a little break, and then let your partner read his or her lists.

Make your plans for your next meeting.

## For Those Working Alone

Since you are working alone, you may find it effective to use John's and Russell's Relationship Graphs as your silent partner. Reread theirs, then look at yours. Notice the similarities and the differences in the undelivered communications. Add more if you can. Be thorough.

## MOVING FROM DISCOVERY TO COMPLETION

Having taken all of the actions suggested in this book so far, you are now ready to take action to complete the loss. Since the loss you're working on occurred, you have probably become familiar with the pain associated with it. Now is the time to complete your relationship with that pain by completing what is unfinished between you and the person you graphed.

At the suggestion of well-meaning friends or professionals, many people write farewell letters to those who have died. Misinformation is the major stumbling block to recovery. Writing a farewell letter, without proper content, is another piece of misinformation. The origin of the concept of writing a farewell letter is buried in antiquity. Over the past half-century, farewell letters have lost their primary motive of completion. Sadly, they often are merely a recitation of events and emotions, much like a newsletter. People who have written such letters report a measure of short-term relief, but no long-term benefit. We've talked with people who wrote a farewell letter but did not take all the actions outlined in this book. All such attempts at completion have been unsuccessful. To be successful, it is essential to convert the work you have done into a *completion* letter rather than a *farewell* letter or newsletter.

## FINAL HOMEWORK ASSIGNMENT: THE GRIEF RECOVERY COMPLETION LETTER©

The Grief Recovery Completion Letter© will help you become complete with everything about the relationship that has been unfinished for you until now. The letter allows you to keep fond memories and all positive aspects of the relationship. You can also keep your beliefs about heaven and other spiritual principles.

You will now be able to say good-bye to what is incomplete. You will be able to say good-bye to any pain you associate with this relationship, including any unmet hopes, dreams, and expectations. You can also say good-bye to the unrealistic expectation of getting something from someone who could not or would not give it. It is most important to remember that good-bye signals the end of this communication, *but that it is not the end of the relationship.*

It is finally time to write your Grief Recovery Completion Letter©. We don't want this letter to be an unsuccessful attempt at recovery for you. It's not a good idea to discuss what you're doing with others. Friends and relatives may mean well, but they haven't read what you've read. They haven't done the work you've done. Please pay close attention to these instructions on what to say and how to proceed.

## General Instructions

Writing the letter is best done alone, and in one complete session. Writing the letter can be an emotionally painful experience, and there is too much temptation to avoid the pain. You've already proven your courage. Use it now to write this letter. Many people have known for a long time what wasn't emotionally complete; they just didn't know what to do about it.

## Specific Instructions

Allow at least an hour. The most effective way to write your letter is to have your Relationship Graph and your lists of apologies, forgiveness, and significant emotional statements in front of you. Look over the graph and the lists and then write your letter. Your graph and lists may contain many repetitions. It is not necessary to repeat the same recovery communications over and over. Use this letter to consolidate them into the most concise expression possible. Your letter should be primarily focused on the recovery categories.

There is no limit on how much you can write, but the emotional intensity is often lost in volume. This is your opportunity to say the most important unsaid things. Generally, two or three standard pages is sufficient. It is okay to write a little more or a little less. If you write more than five pages, you probably need to consider whether you've turned the letter into a newsletter or if you are repeating the same things.

Writing the letter may or may not be an emotional experience for you. Do not be concerned if it is not emotional. Every griever is different and unique.

Here is a helpful format for your letter.

*Dear Dad (use the name or title that best represents how you remember the person),*

*I have been reviewing our relationship, and I have discovered some things that I want to tell you.*

*Dad, I apologize for. . . .*
*Dad, I apologize for. . . .*
*Dad, I apologize for. . . .*

*(You will probably list more than three incomplete communications in this section. It is helpful to keep them grouped by category.)*

*Dad, I forgive you for. . . .*
*Dad, I forgive you for. . . .*
*Dad, I forgive you for. . . .*

*(You will probably list more than three incomplete communications in this section. It is helpful to keep them grouped by category.)*

*Dad, I want you to know . . . (significant emotional statement).*
*Dad, I want you to know . . . (significant emotional statement).*
*Dad, I want you to know . . . (significant emotional statement).*

*(You will probably list more than three incomplete communications in this section. It is helpful to keep them grouped by category.)*

## Closing Your Letter

Grief recovery is about completion. In order to complete what you have discovered, you must end your letter effectively.

When you speak to a friend on the phone, you conclude the conversation with the word *good-bye* to signal the end of the conversation. We conclude our completion letter with *good-bye* to signal the end of this communication.

For the vast majority of grieving people, the most effective and accurate closing is simply: "I love you, I miss you. Good-bye Dad."

However, many of you may have difficulty with "I love you" and "I miss you." If those statements are not truthful for you, do not say them. An effective alternative is: "I have to go now, and I have to let go of the pain. Good-bye Dad."

You can create other closing statements based on your unique relationship. What should remain constant are the very last words, "Good-bye Dad." Failure to say good-bye can often negate all the good work you've done. *It is the good-bye that completes the communication.* Do not substitute other words. Not saying good-bye leaves the communication open and runs the risk of leaving you incomplete.

## Completion Letter—Examples

To help you gain a clear idea of how to write your completion letter, we will give you examples from the relationships we have graphed. The examples are presented in short form to illustrate how to do it. The original letters were longer.

Here are excerpts from John's letter to his younger brother, who died in 1969.

> *Dear Dennis,*
>
> *I have been reviewing our relationship and have discovered some things I want to say.*
>
> *Dennis, I apologize for being so rough on you when you broke my bow and arrow.*
>
> *Dennis, I apologize for acting like a drill instructor the year you lived with me in California.*
>
> *Dennis, I apologize for fighting with you about your getting married.*
>
> *Dennis, I forgive you for wrecking my car.*
>
> *Dennis, I forgive you for the things you did when you lived with me in California, like not taking care of your room, not putting gas in the car, and running up big phone bills.*
>
> *Dennis, I want you to know how much I appreciated the going-away party you and Bruce threw for me. I want you to know how much it meant to me that you told me you loved me. Thank you.*

*Dennis, I want you to know how proud I was of you.*

*Dennis, I want you to know all of the things that I would have said had I known that I would never talk to you again. I want you to know how much I loved you. I want you to know how proud (and envious) I was of your incredible ability to just pick up a guitar and play any song you ever heard. I want you to know how proud I was of your athletic skill, especially the pole vaulting.*

*Dennis, I want you to know how sad I have been, realizing that you were not here to share life with. I would have loved to have seen how your career and family life would have been. I am sad that you did not get to be uncle to my children.*

*Dennis, I love you, I miss you. Good-bye Dennis.*

Here are excerpts from Russell's completion letter to Vivienne.

*Dear Viv,*

*I have been reviewing our relationship and have discovered some things I want to say.*

*Viv, I apologize for being overbearing.*

*Viv, I apologize for not listening to you, and for not hearing what you were trying to tell me.*

*Viv, I apologize that I never told you how much I appreciated your skills, and about the positive things that you contributed to our business. Thank you.*

*Viv, I forgive you for not telling me what was going on with you.*

*Viv, I forgive you for not understanding that I was not ready to have children, and for not waiting for me.*

*Viv, I forgive you for how you ended the relationship.*

*Viv, I want you to know how proud I was to be seen with you.*
*Viv, I want you to know that I am positive that you are a*
*fabulous mother. And, from time to time, I have been sad that*
*you and I did not get to be parents together.*
*Viv, I have to go now,*
*Good-bye Viv.*

## IMPORTANT NOTE

**Communication of a completion letter is a private and confidential issue. As we have stated, forgiveness and negative emotional statements are never made directly to living people. Russell's letter to Vivienne is presented only to illustrate what you must do. A completion letter should never be sent or read to anyone other than your grief recovery partner.**

## FINAL PARTNERS MEETING: READING YOUR LETTER

Begin by reaffirming your commitments to total honesty, absolute confidentiality, and the uniqueness of your individual recovery. As always, meet in a private place where you will not feel uncomfortable if you cry. Have tissues handy.

Undelivered emotional communications must almost always be verbalized and must almost always be heard by another living person to be considered a completed communication. We have known people who have done everything we have asked you to do, but have not read the letter to a living person. We know them, because they have shown up at our seminars still feeling incomplete. Many of them read the letters at a grave site but had not had another living person there to hear it.

Our brains are unique and somewhat stubborn. No matter what our spiritual or religious beliefs may be, our unconscious mind demands a living observer to attest to the completeness of our communication. We are not trying to be intellectual or mystical; it is merely our practical experience with recovering grievers that has taught us what works and what doesn't.

### Instructions for the Listener

1. Your first instruction is to adopt the image of a *heart with ears*. It is your job to listen and listen only. You may laugh or cry if appropriate, but *you must not talk at all*. Nothing about what you do can imply judgment, criticism, or analysis.

2. Take a position at least a few feet away from the reader. We don't want you in the reader's face; it can be a little intimidating. Let your body be relaxed. You are a friend listening to an important communication.

3. During the letter reading, do not touch the reader at all. At this juncture, touch usually stops feelings. We want this reading to be emotional. The reader will have his or her own tissues handy.

4. There is a very real possibility that you will be affected by listening to what your partner reads. Please let that be okay with you. However, you must keep in mind that this is not about you. So, to a limited degree, you need to control the intensity of your reaction. On the other hand, if tears well

up in your eyes, please leave them there. If you wipe them away, you give the message that tears are bad.

5.  Your presence is important to the reader. You must *stay in the moment,* even if your head and your heart want to pull you away. Listen with your heart on behalf of your partner.

6.  As soon as the reader says good-bye, immediately offer a hug. You will have a sense of how long the hug should last. Don't rush it. The letter has been a culmination of some very painful work.

7.  Remember not to analyze, judge, or criticize. It is not necessarily a good idea to talk about the experience. Talking tends to lead to analysis, judgment, or intellectualizing.

**Instructions for the Letter Reader**

1.  Choose a place that is totally safe for you. Avoid public places.

2.  Bring along a box of tissues. There is a high probability that you will experience some strong emotions as you read your letter. Keep the tissues where you can get them. We don't want your listener handing them to you.

3.  Before you start reading your letter, close your eyes. Although you have enlisted the help of a listener, your objective is to read the letter to whom it was written. Get a mental image of the person you are completing with if you can.

4.  Open your eyes. Start reading your letter. You may or may not have an emotional response to your reading. Either way is okay. If you start to choke up, try to talk while you cry. The emotions are contained in the words you have written. Try to push the words up and out of your mouth. Do not swallow your words or your feelings.

5. When you get to the very end, before reading your good-bye sentence, close your eyes, get an image of the person again, and say your final words. This may be accompanied by many tears. If so, make sure you get the words spoken, *especially the good-bye.*

6. Remember, you are saying good-bye to the pain, and you are saying good-bye to any unfinished business. You are *not* saying good-bye to the fond memories. You are *not* saying good-bye to your spiritual beliefs. Say good-bye to the emotional incompleteness. Say good-bye to the pain, isolation, and confusion. Say good-bye to the physical relationship that you had but that has now ended or changed. Say good-bye and then let it be okay that you cry and let it all out. Also, let it be okay if you do not cry. It is essential that you say good-bye or you will probably remain incomplete.

7. As soon as you finish, ask your listener for a hug. You might want and need the hug to be quite long. Don't cut it short. You may find yourself sobbing for a while. Let that be okay with you. You probably have been holding on to the pain for a while. Don't rush the feelings.

**For Those Working Alone**

If you have been working without a partner, we are going to encourage you to find someone "safe" to help you, someone who would be willing to listen to your letter. The safe person could be a friend, a family member, a therapist, a clergy person—anyone to whom you could explain some simple guidelines. When you find a willing listener, show him or her the listener's instructions in this chapter. Ask your listener whether he or she is willing and able to follow them exactly. Also ask for a commitment to absolute confidentiality.

Some people never find anyone with whom they feel safe. We do not want to compound the problem by telling you to do something that you cannot or will not do.

If you must read the letter without a living human witness, go ahead. Reading a letter alone to a memento, a picture, or at a grave site, can have value. One helpful idea is to read your letter to a tape recorder. Don't destroy the letter. You might find someone you feel safe with to read it to at a future date.

## WHAT DOES COMPLETION MEAN?

Having taken all of the actions and having read your letter, you are 100 percent complete. Completion means that you have discovered and communicated what was unfinished for you in all aspects of the relationship that you have remembered up to this moment. It does not mean that you will never be sad again, any more than you would never be happy again. Completion allows you to return to a full range of human emotions. It means that you don't have to go over the same things again and again.

In your day-to-day life, there will be many reminders of the one who has died or your partner from a marriage that has failed. Your moment-to-moment thoughts and feelings will come with emotions attached. Some of your feelings will be happy, fond, and joyful. Some will be negative, sad, and uncomfortable. This is normal. Do not fight it, just allow it. *If you allow negative feelings to occur without resistance, they will pass.* If you try to hide or bury them, they may become painful.

We suggest that you process every feeling in the moment you have it. But what does this mean and how do you do it?

Imagine that you are standing by a large window next to a giant fish tank at a place like Sea World. You are standing there with a friend, watching the fish glide by. As each fish passes, you have a reaction. First, an incredibly beautiful blue fish swims by. Its fins are like silk gently pushing side to side. You turn to your friend and say, "Wow, have you ever seen anything so gorgeous in your life?" Almost before you finish your question, a massive shark swims into view, jagged teeth glinting in the water. Instinctively, you clutch your heart and step back as if the shark could actually get at you. You say to your friend, "How terrifying! My heart is beating like a drum." And just then a school of teeny silver fish, each hardly as big as your little finger, swarms past. There seem to be at least a thousand of them. They twist and turn as a group, in unison, as if only one brain were controlling them. You are fascinated, and you say, "How do all of them know how to go the same way? How come they don't bump into each other?"

You have just processed every feeling in the moment you had it. In the first picture, you were awed by the beauty of the blue fish. In the second, you were frightened by the shark and the images of destruction it conjured in your mind. And lastly, you were baffled and amazed by the synchronized flow of the school in motion.

In each case, you experienced the feeling, verbalized it, and then moved to the next one. In the fish tank analogy, the movement of the fish keeps you going from one feeling to the next. Sometimes in real life we get stuck on a feeling. Or we keep bringing ourselves back to a feeling we had some time ago. When you become aware that you are looking backward at old feelings, remind yourself to keep watching the fish and respond to the next feeling that arises.

## STUCK ON A PAINFUL IMAGE

One of the most painful of all experiences is to have a loved one die violently. You may have seen the accident or the aftermath. You may have seen photos of the scene. Or you may only have the pictures your imagination has conjured up. In any event, for many people the imagery seems constant, as if it will never cease. Some of you may have equally disturbing images of your loved one's final hours, days, or weeks as they struggled through a terminal illness. The devastating nature of some diseases often alters appearance so much that you hardly recognize someone you have known your entire life.

Most people, in trying to help a friend, will tell them not to think about it. That is very nearly impossible. We think it is more helpful to acknowledge that the images and pictures are indeed horrible and painful. We also believe that the griever needs to be reminded that they have many thousands of other images as well.

Death is not always a gentle slipping away, and is often difficult to watch. A woman tells us of her husband's final night at the hospital, with vivid details. Our response is, "What a horrible final picture that is for you." Then we ask, "Do you remember the first time you saw the man who became your husband?" She says yes, and we say, "Tell us what he looked like that day." And she does.

We all have tens of thousands of images of our loved ones. Some of the images are wonderful and happy. Some are negative and sad. And sometimes the final ones are very

painful, as when violence or disease have altered how someone looked. It is unrealistic to tell someone not to remember
what they saw or imagined. By acknowledging the discomfort of the final, unpleasant pictures, we allow the remembering of all the other pictures. Each time the ending
pictures crop up, they must be acknowledged.

Acknowledging the painful pictures and remembering others does not deny or minimize the painful ones.
When grievers are allowed and encouraged to state what
they are experiencing, the painful pictures subside more
quickly. This leaves more room for the review of the entire relationship, not just the ending.

## WHAT ABOUT NEW DISCOVERIES? COLE'S WINDOW STORY

Here is one of our favorite stories for illustrating how to complete your relationship to new discoveries.

When John's son Cole was eight years old, he and his pals
would play baseball in the front yard. John taught the boys to
position themselves sideways along the front of the house, so
that if they missed the ball, it would not break a window. All
went well until one fine day the little boys forgot. Cole un-
leashed one and smash went the neighbor's picture window.

Upon arriving home, John asked Cole to tell him the truth
about the window. Cole explained, as only an eight-year-old
can, how the ball happened to break the window. Honking
horns, barking dogs, and flashing sunlight all contributed to

the drama—plus the fact that Cole and his buddies had forgotten to play across the front of the house rather than toward it.

In the middle of the story, John realized that he had stopped listening and started planning Cole's punishment in his mind. Alarmed by his own thoughts, John asked Cole to take a break and go out and play for a while. John looked heavenward and asked this question: "God, where would I get the idea that I want my son, whom I love, to associate telling me the truth with getting punished?" And in a flash, John had his answer. The image of John's dad popped up in his mind's eye as clear as crystal.

John realized that he had just discovered another piece of unfinished emotional business with his own father. He got a pad and pen and wrote:

*Dad, I was just listening to my son, who I adore more than I can say. He is one of the grandchildren you never got to meet. As he told me the truth about an event with a ball and a window, I stopped listening to him and started preparing his punishment. But that didn't feel right to me. So I have been doing some soul searching. I have just had a revelation—that by the time I was his age, I had long since stopped telling you the truth. Every time I told you the truth, you punished me, and you punished me hard and hurtfully.*

*Dad, I do not want my son to associate truth with punishment. I have to break the cycle set up by what you did to me. I have to forgive you for hurting me every time I told you the truth. I forgive you so I can be free to do things differently with my son. I forgive you so I can be totally free to tell the truth and live the truth and encourage my son to do the same.*

*I have to go now. I love you. Good-bye Dad.*

Having written the letter to his dad, John felt free to talk to Cole about the consequences of his actions. He helped Cole apologize to the neighbor for the broken window and set up a program where Cole and his pals could earn some money to pay for the window. There was no punishment. But John needed to take one more action to be emotionally complete with the event. The next morning John read the letter to his dad out loud so Russell could hear it, and then got a hug from Russell. John completed the communication by having a living person hear the words. We take the same completion actions we teach you. Each new discovery needs to be completed and verbalized to make room for the next piece to float up to the surface.

## MORE HELP WITH RELATIONSHIP GRAPHS AND COMPLETION LETTERS

Now that you've done at least one Relationship Graph and Grief Recovery Completion Letter©, you can apply those actions to other losses. This edition contains new material under the heading *More on Choices and Other Losses*, which begins on page 167. You'll find guidance on losses that relate to:

Death of parent when you were young

Absence of a parent through divorce, adoption

Infant loss, infertility

Loved ones with Alzheimer's or dementia

Growing up in an alcoholic or otherwise dysfunctional home (addresses intangible losses of trust, safety, and childhood)

Losses related to religious faith, health, career, moving

Taking action on all of the losses that have affected you enhances the benefits you get from using this book.

# 13

# *What Now?*

Having taken the action of completion, you've still got more work to do.

Making a Loss History Graph may have alerted you to the fact that you have a few more incomplete relationships to work on. We suggest that you start immediately. Our goal for you is the emotional freedom that results from completion of all prior loss experiences.

Make a list of the relationships that you think are still incomplete. Most people have three or four relationships that can benefit from this process. Remember, your relationships with living people are affected when you remain incomplete. If you have worked with a partner, it is helpful to continue with that person.

The process is much quicker the second time through. You do not have to do a Loss History Graph again. You can start with the Relationship Graph. Remember to reaffirm the commitments to honesty, confidentiality, and uniqueness.

After completing the other incomplete relationships, it is

time to live your life. The principles and actions of grief recovery are your new tool kit for losses, disappointments, and other painful life experiences. Practice them so that they become a new habit.

## CLEANUP WORK

After completion, we gain a new perspective. Things look different because we have changed on the inside. Completing our relationship has brought about this change. Since the inside has changed, it will now be necessary to look at the outside. You'll want to adjust your environment to reflect this new inside perspective on the loss.

The first step in your cleanup work will be to look at outside reminders of the loss. Earlier we referred to grievers who hold on to everything that represents the deceased loved one. We called this enshrinement. We hold on to these things when we're emotionally incomplete with the loss. There will now be no need to hold on to all of these objects. Some of the objects won't seem to fit with your new perspective; these are the ones you'll want to dispose of. It is normal to want to keep some things and not be sure about others.

Perhaps helpful friends have told you to just get rid of it all—clothes, mementos, everything. But most of us don't want to get rid of it all. One woman we met told us a story of how she made a mistake in disposing of her husband's effects. Everyone kept telling her she had to get rid of all his things. She wanted to do what was right. So one day she drank four bottles of beer to get up the courage to do the job. In her half-drunken state, she threw away everything. She regretted this action the very next day, but by then it was too late.

Before you rush out and throw everything away, let's make a plan that will work. *When possible, never do any of these chores alone.*

### Disposing of Clothes: The Pile Plan

One of the most painful tasks for grievers is deciding what to do with the clothes. One good approach has been called the ABC Plan. This approach can also be used for other personal belongings. It has also been lovingly referred to as the Pile Plan. You'll see why as we go along.

Remember, the objective is to end up with what you want to keep without keeping things you don't need or want. Take all the clothes and put them in the living room. Do we mean physically move all the clothes? Yes, that's exactly what we mean. Go through them one at a time. Make three piles of clothes. If you want to talk about a memory that one of the articles stimulates for you, please do so with the person helping you, or call someone. The piles should be grouped as follows:

> Pile A contains the things you are certain you want to keep.
>
> Pile B contains the things you are certain you want to dispose of. Things to sell. Things to give to other family members. Things to give to charity or the church.
>
> Pile C contains all those things you're not sure about yet. If there is any doubt at all about which pile an item goes in, it goes in pile C.

We are not in a race. We're employing a clear plan that works. As you stand in the room looking at all the clothes, it may dawn on you why some people refer to this as the Pile Plan. Dispose of the piles as follows:

> Put pile A back in the closet.
> Give pile B to individuals, groups, and so on.
> Load pile C into bags and boxes and take them to the garage or the attic.

Then congratulate yourself and thank your friend. One month later, bring all the pile C bags and boxes back into the living room and work the plan all over again. Once again, never work alone! Pile A is for the few things you find that you want to keep. Pile B is for those things you are sure you want to discard. Everything else goes back into the bags and boxes, and back into the garage or attic. Doing this task one more time will accomplish your goal of keeping what you want to keep and not retaining things you don't need. If necessary, do it all over again in three months. Eventually, you will be done.

**The New Account Solution**

Another problem people have trouble with is the checking account with their loved one's name on it. It's fine if you don't want to change the account name. Yet many spouses find that changing the name generates a desired feeling of independence. Once again, people often attack this problem from the wrong direction. Instead of taking your loved one's name off the checking account, open a new one with just your name. Each month, make sure some of your transactions are done through the new account. In no time at all, you'll have a new pattern established and the old checks will no longer be a constant reminder of the loss. To open the new account, go to the bank with a friend, never alone.

## Dealing with Anniversary Dates

Even after all the work you've done, certain occasions will still make you sad. This is because you established a lot of familiar habits with your loved one. The good news is that these times are usually predictable. We call them anniversary dates. They don't stand for conventional anniversaries only. Any day that had significant meaning for you can be considered an anniversary date. Since we almost always know when they're coming, we can prepare for them.

The problem is in keeping your feelings to yourself. There is the temptation to try to handle these sad days alone. Don't do that. It's normal for recovered grievers to feel sad on anniversary dates.

## Celebrity Deaths

In the aftermath of the death of Diana, Princess of Wales, our phones were very busy. Many calls were from grievers whose hearts were broken. Many were requests for interviews by national and international media to help them understand the incredible outpouring of grief.

The constant question was, "Why do people have so much feeling about someone they never knew?" The answer: *They did know her, they just never met her.*

If you will recall, in our comments about the death of a child, we talked about having an emotional relationship with someone we had not yet physically met. We all have emotional relationships with the people we admire. They may be princesses, baseball players, actors, or ballerinas. We all have fantasies of meeting them and spending time with them. We usually never get to meet them, and most of us never write a fan letter. When they die, we are left with some undelivered emotional communications.

Since it is a one-way relationship, you probably do not need to do a Relationship Graph. But write a completion letter. Tell the deceased person how much you appreciated him or her. Tell the person that you are sad you never met so that you could have said so in person. Remember to close your letter with "I love you (if appropriate), I will miss you, Good-bye." If possible, read your letter to a friend.

# PART FOUR

# More on Choices and Other Losses

In response to many inquiries over the years, we are pleased to present some additional material that will enhance your ability to deal with the losses that have affected your life. This new part contains two sections.

The first section is **More on Choices,** which gives expanded help on choosing which loss to work on first.

The second section is **Guidelines for Working on Specific Losses**, which contains information on losses related to:

> Death of parent when you were young
> Absence of a parent through divorce, adoption
> Infant loss, infertility
> Loved ones with Alzheimer's or dementia
> Growing up in an alcoholic or otherwise dysfunctional home (addresses intangible losses of trust, safety, and childhood)
> Losses related to religious faith, career, health, moving

# 14

# More on Choices—
# Which Loss to Work on First

Choosing which loss to work on first is more important than it might seem at first glance. Even though the loss that brought you to this book may have happened recently, and may be causing you a great deal of pain, it isn't always the best first choice. The best way to explain it is to ask the question: "If you were going to build a house, would you put the roof on first? And if so, what would hold the roof up?" Using the obvious answers to those questions, we often suggest that people go back and work on their foundational relationships, even if those relationships are not the current cause of pain. There is real benefit from working on those relationships first because elements of them will have been carried forward and affected your more recent relationships.

## START WITH RELATIONSHIPS YOU REMEMBER

It is not uncommon for people to arrive at this book because of the death of a parent when they were very young, or as a consequence of a family split-up that resulted in the long-term loss of contact with one or both parents. Still others, who were adopted at an early age, may feel incomplete because they don't know their birth parents. While the death or absence of a parent, or the mysteries surrounding adoption, may be a defining event in someone's life, it is almost never the correct place to start taking the actions of Grief Recovery.

There are many reasons not to start with the death of a parent, or with other losses of contact. The most obvious relates to your age when the death or family break-up happened. If the loss happened between your birth and age 6, you will have a limited amount of conscious memories of the missing parent and the relationship you had with them. The things that happened to you in the first few years of your life, especially prior to the dawn of conscious memory, are difficult to access with any degree of accuracy. It is almost impossible to create a realistic Relationship Graph of memories that are buried beneath your conscious awareness. It is also dangerous to rely on other people's opinions or reports about things that happened before you can remember.

We suggest you work first on your relationships with those people about whom you have the most conscious memories. Generally speaking that will be the parent(s) who raised you. We are in no way diminishing the likelihood that the death or absence of a parent may be the loss that most affected your life. It's just that we've seen too many people fail when they try to graph their relationship with someone they can hardly remember, before they have learned the techniques of Grief Recovery. What tends to happen is a simple recitation of how bad they have always felt about the absence of that person from their life.

Making Relationship Graphs and writing Completion Letters about those relationships with people you really knew will help you in many ways. It will help you discover and complete what is emotionally incomplete in those relationships. This is true whether the relationships were good, poor, or mixed, and whether or not those people are still living. It will have great benefit for you later when you do the work on the parent who was missing from your life.

As you do this work, it's helpful to remember that in most of the situations where there was the death of a parent, the surviving parent was also grieving. The same is true for both partners in a divorce. It's not unreasonable to suggest that your grieving parent(s) had limited knowledge about dealing with their own grief, as well as limited ability to help you deal with your emotions about the loss. Children learn by observing what their parents do. As you look back, you might realize you were copying one or both of your parents. Some of what they did may have been helpful in terms of communicating about grief, but it's likely that much of what they did and didn't say or show, may have limited your ability to deal with the loss. It is helpful to recognize what you learned from them, so you can discard what is not helpful and take effective actions to complete your grief.

## OTHER FIRST CHOICE CONCERNS: HIDDEN OR DISGUISED CHOICES

On page 113, in the fourth choosing instruction, we indicated that the person/relationship that would be the best for you to work on first may not even appear on your Loss History Graph. It's not uncommon for an alcoholic or otherwise difficult parent to appear on the graph because they caused so much disruption in your life. The hidden loss is often your relationship with your other parent, who may not appear on your graph, especially if he or she is still living. While it might not be obvious, the other parent often represents a huge incomplete relationship. This happens in part because that other parent is often much more present in your life, and because their own grief reactions to their difficult spouse may cause them to create problems for you. The fireworks associated with the problem parent may grab more attention as you reflect on your life, but it is often the other parent that is the best "first" relationship graph for you to choose.

### Death of Spouse or Divorce—Begin at the Beginning

Some people are drawn to this book by the recent death of a spouse. But if you've already done the preliminary work in this book, you may realize that you also have one or more incomplete relationships with your parents or other people who have affected your life. It can benefit you to go back and work on your relationships with your parents before you work on your relationship with your spouse who died. When you work on those earlier relationships, you will discover things that will be valuable later when you work on your relationship with your spouse. Keep in mind that what you brought into your marriage was the product of a great deal that you learned from your parents—or in reaction to them.

The same idea holds true if you were originally drawn to this book because of a recent divorce or romantic ending. It is especially valuable for you to go back and deal with some of your foundational relationships, which will give you greater clarity about your part in the romantic relationship that ended. It will help you be more honest about yourself within the relationship as opposed to being totally focused on what your former spouse did or didn't do that affected the marriage. In effect, it will help you see what emotional baggage you brought to the marriage.

It is entirely your choice which loss you work on first, but always give yourself the option of going back and working on your earliest relationships first. Keep in mind that ultimately you will want to take Grief Recovery actions in all the major relationships with people who affected your life.

# 15

# Guidelines for Working on Specific Losses

## DEATH OR ABSENCE OF PARENT FROM AN EARLY AGE

If you experienced the death or absence of a parent when you were young, we hope you have done as we suggested and made Relationship Graphs and Completion Letters about your relationships to the people who raised you. If so, you are now ready to tackle your relationship with the parent who died or who disappeared from your life.

The guidelines for making a Relationship Graph, converting it into recovery categories, and writing a Completion Letter are still appropriate. The instructions for the Relationship Graph are on pages 129–133. Please go back and re-read the instructions before you start. (For those of you who were adopted, you can use the same guidelines for working on your relationship with the birth parents you never knew.)

Earlier in this book we mentioned that grieving people tend to create larger than life memory pictures in which they either enshrine or bedevil a person who died. There is a tendency for young children who have a parent die, or disappear from their lives, to create huge fantasies about that parent, almost always positive ones. Since there is such a strong inclination to enshrine (or sometimes bedevil) a missing parent, we want to repeat one specific instruction from page 132: "To maintain truth and accuracy and avoid enshrinement or bedevilment, we recommend that you have at least two events above the line and at least two events below the line." We suggest this so you'll be able to create the most accurate memory picture of your relationship to that parent.

Many people tell the painful story of their loss over and over. They don't realize that reciting a general litany of unhappiness is one of the main reasons they stay stuck. There are two important keys to success in becoming emotionally complete with the parent who died or left. The first is to focus on the specific events and non-events you recall, and the emotions you had and may still have about them. This will help you move away from "storytelling," which keeps you trapped. The other is to avoid an intellectual analysis of what happened to you as the result of the death or absence.

### Starting Your Graph

Your Relationship Graph about the missing parent begins with the first memory you have of that parent, assuming you have such a memory. There is a possibility that you have no memories about that parent. As sad as that may be, you have to be truthful about it. You may have heard stories or seen pictures, but if you have no actual memories, you will use your dawn-of-concious-memory (see page 99) as the start place for your Relationship Graph.

One of the obstacles in graphing your relationship to someone who was not there involves things that did not happen. In order to overcome the fact that things that might or should have happened didn't, it's helpful to remember a first recital or soccer game and your missing parent was not there. You may have been very aware of that absence. You may have felt different from the other kids because they had both parents. You may not have felt safe to talk about it with the parent who was raising you, and you may have thought that if you did, you would be too sad. This kind of thing may have happened many times at important events in your young life, and you may have had tons of feelings about the missing parent, but those feelings may have gotten trapped inside you. Keep in mind, those feelings were not limited to childhood events. Many sad memories are about graduations or wedding days that are affected by the absence of the parent who would naturally have been at the significant events later in your life.

It's also possible that after a while, you learned to push those kinds of feelings away, and it almost seemed like you were not bothered by the fact that your other parent was not there. What's more than likely true, is that no matter how good you got at pushing feelings away, you were still being affected. One of the primary purposes for taking the actions of Grief Recovery is to become complete with what was unfinished so you won't have to push feelings away anymore.

Create your Relationship Graph about the missing parent by looking back at specific events and your emotional responses to them. There's an almost unlimited range of things that did and did not happen in relationship to the missing parent that may have affected your life. Here's a short sample list:

- birthdays and other holidays
- first lost tooth

- first day of school
- music recitals, sports events
- first boyfriend or girlfriend
- arguments with custodial parent

Of course as you got older, the kinds of things that happened may have been different, but the feelings of not having that missing parent there to share them with you can still be very strong.

### From Relationship Graph to Recovery Categories and Then to Completion Letter

After you finish your graph from as far back as you remember right up to the present, it is time to convert what you've put on the graph into the recovery categories—apologies, forgiveness, and significant emotional statements. Please go back and reread the instructions for converting your Relationship Graph entries into the recovery categories, on pages 136–143.

**In addition to those instructions, please understand that each negative significant emotional statement you make must be accompanied by a forgiveness. If not, you are simply reciting pain without completion. Many people make the painful statement but skip the forgiveness and leave themselves emotionally incomplete. An example would be: "Mom, by not taking care of your health, you took yourself away from me. In many ways, your absence made my life miserable." In order to become emotionally complete, it's helpful to add, "And I forgive you for that so I can be free."**

After you convert your graph entries into recovery categories, it is time to write your Completion Letter. Use the instructions on pages 145–151. Stick with the format. It will work perfectly well on this relationship, as it has on the others. When you have finished the work, get together with a listening partner (preferably the same person you've been working with) so you can read your graph and letter. Use the reader-listener instructions on pages 152–154.

## INFANT LOSS AND INFERTILITY

If you had a child die or if you have not been able to have children, please go back and read pages 130–131. It is a special section called DAWN OF MEMORY—THE DEATH OF AN INFANT. It will help you understand how to start the process of graphing your relationship to a child you conceived, but who was never born, or was stillborn, or was born and lived a very short time. While this may seem focused on a mother, the process also works for fathers who have their own emotions about the things that might have happened different or better, and their own unique hopes, dreams, and expectations about the relationship they were going to have with that child.

The general guidelines we outlined in the previous section about the death or absence of a parent apply in this situation also, since you are graphing someone you didn't get a chance to know, even though you had established an emotional relationship with him or her. This last applies to infertility even when there's never been a pregnancy. We establish relationships to the child we want, and about whom we have hopes and dreams. It is important to "grieve and complete" your relationship to the dream of having your own child. This will allow you to make another choice, possibly that of adoption. You can also choose not to adopt, but the point is that you must first become as complete as possible with your earlier dreams, so that you can make new choices.

Some people who conceived a child who was never born or didn't live were never guided to name the baby. The Relationship Graph and Completion Letter give you an opportunity to name the baby that you had developed a relationship with. The same is true for those dealing with infertility. There's no reason you can't name the baby you've dreamed of having. While you may not have conceived, you certainly had a relationship with the baby that that you hoped to have. Giving that baby a name may help you with your graph and letter.

## ALZHEIMER'S—DEMENTIA

One of the most painful things to endure is the slipping away of someone important to us, especially when they look and sound like the person we know them to be. The classic story involves a mom who descends into the strange world of Alzheimer's or dementia, leaving her adult daughter in a limbo of her own. In the beginning, the mom may occasionally forget her daughter's name and other details about her. As the mom continues slipping away, the daughter keeps trying to get mom to be the way she used to be. But that cannot happen. What does happen is that the situation gets worse. Eventually, it turns into, "You seem to be a nice young lady, what's your name?"

As the condition worsens, the daughter gets more and more frustrated, and eventually stops visiting her mom at the nursing home, because it's just too hard for her to see. A year after her last visit, the daughter gets a call from the nursing home that her mother has died. The sadness of mom's death is compounded by the daughter's regrets at having left mom at the nursing home to die alone. This is an avoidable tragedy—at least the part about leaving mom, lost and alone, at the nursing home.

Of course the best time for action is as soon as you become aware that someone important to you is in the early stages of Alzheimer's or dementia. But you can do the Relationship Graph and Completion Letter at any time, using the instructions on pages 115–154. While the graphing process doesn't change, the key is to separate your graph into two distinct parts. The first part is your relationship with the person from as far back as you can recall, right up until the onset of the condition that keeps them from being how they were. Write a Completion Letter on that relationship. When you get to the "good-bye" part of your letter, remember that you are saying good-bye to the relationship you had right up until that moment, so you can start a new one based on the changes that are happening with the other person.

In the second section, you will graph your relationship with the changed person. There may be a lot of frustrating events and attached emotions. You might need to make some apologies if you have been less than tolerant and understanding of what's going on with the other person. You also may need to issue a lot of forgiveness for the way that person has talked or acted toward you. And there will probably be some painful emotional statements regarding how difficult it is for you to watch this person slip away from you.

If you have already done a Relationship Graph and Completion Letter about that person, start your new graph at the onset of your awareness of the condition. The freedom you will gain from taking the actions to complete the old relationship will allow you to continue to spend time with the person you love, even though she is no longer the way you knew her.

## GROWING UP IN AN ALCOHOLIC OR OTHERWISE DYSFUNCTIONAL HOME

Growing up in an alcoholic or otherwise dysfunctional home, or where one or both parents have a mental illness, is a major loss. Don't limit yourself to working only on the alcoholic or mentally ill person. We encourage you to look at all of the people involved in your home life and make separate Relationship Graphs and Completion Letters for each person, following the graph and letter instructions from pages 129–154.

**Intangible Losses**

We know that some awful things happen in abusive homes, and with that can come several intangible losses. Here are a few examples: *loss of normalcy*—being forced to endure and cope with things that make no sense at all, especially to a child; *loss of trust*—a child cannot retain a sense of trust in a crazy environment; *loss of safety*—the irrationality associated with alcohol abuse or mental illness makes safety impossible. One of the biggest losses from having been subject to situations with alcohol or mental illness is an overall sense of the *loss of childhood*. You might perceive all of those losses.

It's also likely that they have continued to affect you, especially in intimate relationships that are based on trust and safety. Unfortunately, you cannot get complete with those intangible losses simply by becoming aware that they exist. You will have to do some more work so you can rebuild the sense of trust and safety that you may have had when you were very young, but have lost along the way. (Note: Any or all of those intangible losses can also happen in what appears to be a "normal" home.)

As you start converting each Relationship Graph into the recovery categories, keep the idea of those intangible losses in mind. You will need to use the Significant Emotional Statement and Forgiveness categories to communicate most of them. An example would be: "Dad, I could never bring any of my friends home because of your drinking. I never felt safe and I couldn't trust that you wouldn't embarrass me. I never felt like I was part of a normal home. As I look back, having to always be on alert, it's like I never had a childhood. I forgive you so I can be free." Those few sentences address all of the intangible losses we've mentioned.

We've indicated that people sometimes only focus on the alcoholic and lose sight of the influence of the other parent, who may have impacted them in different ways. In a setting where it was unsafe to bring friends home because Dad was always drunk, it might also have been Mom's responses that were an equal or bigger problem. A communication to Mom might be: "Mom, your reactions to Dad and his drinking were so frantic that I lived as if a nuclear bomb were about to go off any moment. I could never relax, and even as an adult, I have found it difficult not to be on constant high-alert even when nothing in my situation is unsafe. I forgive you for instilling in me a constant sense of dread and doom. I forgive you so I can be free."

## UNIQUE LOSS GRAPHING SITUATIONS: FAITH, CAREER, HEALTH, MOVING

Over the years, we're often asked about creating Relationship Graphs for losses that don't seem to fit conveniently under the obvious headings such as death and divorce. Among the most common are questions about how to graph your relationship to *loss of faith, loss or change of career, or loss or change of health and even to moving.* It may seem as if those losses are more related to ourselves than to other people. But as we show you how to address them, you'll see that they bear a great deal of correlation to the people who are or have been important in your life.

We're about to start showing you how to deal with some of the losses we've just mentioned. But—and make that a capital letter BUT—before you attempt to complete your relationship to any of these other losses, you must take all the actions laid out earlier in this book. This is especially important in relationship to the people who most directly affected your life. Absent that foundational work, attempts at completion of these other kinds of losses tend to be intellectual and analytical. However, if you follow our guidance, you can achieve the greatest degree of emotional completion with any losses that affect your life.

This section addresses three major life areas: faith, health, and career. The first one, on loss of faith, is very thorough. Even though you may not have a loss of faith issue, please read the loss of faith section. It will give you a template for either of the other areas, health and career, that follow.

## Loss of Faith

There are two common ways in which you might feel you've experienced a loss of faith in God or in your religion. One is a specific tragic event that caused a breach of faith that you associate primarily with God. The other is a cumulative loss of faith over a long period of time, often associated not only with God, but with the tenets of your religion, the clergy, your family, and others associated with your church. Your realization of that loss may have been the result of the latest in a succession of disappointments you related to God, or to the principles and people involved.

Whatever caused your loss of faith, we will show you how to complete what was left emotionally unfinished for you. With those tools you can become emotionally complete with God, and with any of the people, events, or institutions that caused or contributed to your loss of faith. You will start by making a Relationship Graph about your faith. The graph will help you identify which elements relate directly to God, and which relate to the people you associate with your breach or loss of faith. The faith graph is a collection of mini-Relationship Graphs with the people who affected that part of your life, as well as with God.

*Review Graphing Instructions*—Before you start your graph, go back and review chapter 11, from pages 115–133, on how to make a Relationship Graph. As you recall events and people, put positive or happy experiences above the graph line, and negative or painful ones below the line. In some of the events you recall, your reactions will be about what did or didn't happen and how it affected your relationship with God, both positively and negatively. Add the names of any people involved, and the approximate year the events happened. Don't be preoccupied if you don't remember some names, dates, or exact details.

Start your graph by going back to your earliest memories that relate to religion. That will include:

- your parents
- priests, rabbis, or ministers (the clergy)
- Sunday school and Sunday school teachers
- church, temple, or mosque (from now on we'll just use church)
- the tenets of your church

At some point you probably started learning the doctrines of your religion. You may have liked what you were learning, or maybe not. You may have gone through periods of time when you questioned them. If you had strong thoughts and feelings about those religious and spiritual principles, put them on your graph. There's a high probability they are part of what has affected you. A complaint we've heard is that during childhood, some children observe church leaders not following the precepts they teach. If you had that experience, it might have been part of a loss of trust that contributed to your loss of faith, if not in God, then in the people who were teaching you about God. Also important is whether or not you told anyone about what you experienced, and whether that person said or did anything to help you. All of that is part of your relationship to your faith and should appear on your Relationship Graph.

When you finish the graph, you will convert what you have discovered into the three recovery categories—apologies, forgiveness, and significant emotional statements. To review how to do that, go back and re-read chapter 12, from page 136 to 143. As you convert each of the things on your graph into one or more of the recovery categories, you will see which ones you need to direct at God, and which ones need to be directed at the people involved. Take your time and devote some energy into converting your discoveries into the appropriate categories. The more thoroughly you do that, the more effective your Completion Letter will be.

There may be some people with whom you had limited relationships, but to whom you feel grateful for their influence or guidance related to religious matters. There may be no need for apologies or forgiveness, just a desire to say "thank you," which is a simple but powerful emotional statement.

*Review Letter Writing Instructions*—After you've finished

converting your graph into the recovery categories, it's time to write your Grief Recovery Completion Letter©. Before you start your letter, go back and review the letter writing instructions that begin on the bottom of page 145 and continue through page 151. Pay particular attention to the top of page 147, which will remind you to consolidate recurring elements of your graph so you don't repeat them in your letter. Then take your edited list of comments in the recovery categories and convert them into your Completion Letter. Keeping in mind that this letter will be addressed to many people as well as God, it's a good idea to start each comment with the person's name if you remember it. Using the name will help you distinguish who your comment is aimed at, and later, will add valuable emotion when you read your letter aloud.

Since you have things to say to many people, in addition to God, you will have a letter that is aimed in multiple directions. It will encompass all of the people and relationships that appeared on your graph, including God. It is like a tree with many branches, with each of the people and events involved as part of the whole picture. We recommend that you start the letter with a variation on the phrase we suggested for the beginning of your other Completion Letters. In this case you would say, "I have been reviewing my relationship to my faith and to God, and to the people who have been associated with my religious experiences along the way, and I've discovered some things I need to say."

There's a high probability that your first entries will have to do with your parents, which would be the earliest entries that appeared on your graph. Here are some possible statements when your early memories are positive: "Mom, thank you so much for teaching me about God and heaven. I can remember as a little child feeling safe in knowing those things you told me. Mom, thanks for taking me to Sunday school and encouraging me to read the Bible."

On the other hand, if your earliest memories are not positive, you might say: "Mom, I forgive you for forcing me to go to Sunday school. The teacher was really mean and scared me about what would happen if I didn't believe what she said. And, Mom, I forgive you for not helping me when I told you about that."

Those are simple examples at the positive and negative ends. Your memories may not be as concrete on one side or the other. They might be a mixture. And you might have had different feelings related to Dad than you had to Mom. You can make your comments individual to each of your parents in the letter format.

The next entry in your letter might be to a Sunday school teacher, about whom you had either positive, negative, or mixed feelings. Make your statements about those feelings in the appropriate categories. As we said, you may or may not remember names or dates, but don't let that stop you. The point is to deliver the undelivered emotional communications, indirectly, to people who affected you in one way or another as they relate to your religious beliefs. You may have thanked your teacher or clergy member when something happened years ago, but you may now feel a need to express something a little stronger that might sound like this: "Pastor Joey, I want you to know how much your teachings helped me later in life, and how much they affected the way I talked about these matters to my own children. Thank you." The same style would be used when you have something negative to say, but it would have to contain forgiveness. Example: "Mr. Glazer, I remember being very scared when you taught about the devil. That fear has stayed with me much of my life. I forgive you so I can be free to let that fear go."

We should mention here that many people feel angry at God, especially when something bad has happened to them or to someone important to them. You may be angry at God, but you might be uncomfortable with that feeling. You may need to forgive God, but you might be fearful of the idea of "forgiving" God, as if that would be disrespectful. The problem is that if you are harboring a resentment against God for things that did or did not happen, then you must forgive or you will never be able to rebuild your trust in God. Even if a renewed faith in God is not your goal, there is no value in walking around with a resentment burning in your heart and soul.

On the other hand, you may have some very important positive things to communicate. In those instances where you believe that God has been with you through something difficult, you might say: "God, thank you for walking with me and my family as we struggled with the deaths of our cousins in the car accident." That's a generic way of saying it. Use your own beliefs and your own language to say what's important for you.

We know that there are many different beliefs about communicating with God, and we are not suggesting that anyone do anything they feel uncomfortable with. With that warning in mind, we recommend that you say both positive and negative things to God as directly as possible, whether they are apologies, forgiveness, or significant emotional statements. The more directly you communicate those ideas and feelings, the more complete you will feel.

*Closing Your Letter*—The closing, like the salutation, is usually aimed at many people as well as God. There are as many correct ways to close this letter as there are individual people. We cannot stress enough how important it is to say good-bye at the end of this letter, like all other Completion Letters. Yes, we are suggesting that you say good-bye to God and to everyone else the letter is directed to. But remember that good-bye does not signal the end of the relationship; it signals the end of this communication. One method is to issue a general comment that is aimed at everyone involved, which might look like this: "I have to go now, and I have to let go of any pain I have associated with God, with religion, and with any of the people involved. Good-bye." Or you might want to aim your closing to God and to a few select individuals. That's fine; it's your choice. Just remember to say good-bye at the very end.

After you have written your Grief Recovery Completion Letter©, the last piece of the puzzle is to read it, out loud, to a safe person. Use the Instructions for Listeners and Readers on pages 152–154. It is essential that your listener make a commitment to absolute confidentiality regarding the letter you read to them.

### Loss of Career—Career Changes

The format for dealing with career issues follows the same general outline we just demonstrated for dealing with faith issues. If you did not read the last section, please go back and do so. It will make the following instructions easier.

Your relationship to your career issues starts with your very first chores as a child. That assumes that you had some chores, but if you didn't, that's important too. You may have gotten an allowance that correlated to chores. If so, that goes on the graph. You will also start remembering and noting what you saw your parents doing—or not—as it relates to work. Were they steady or not? Did they demonstrate a good "work ethic"? If you came from a home where only Dad worked, did Mom take her household tasks seriously and thereby show you by example how to get things done? If Mom worked and Dad stayed home, the same question applies. All of the observations you made in your childhood, good or bad, contribute to what you believe and how you feel as it relates to work or career.

Fill in your graph chronologically, moving from childhood through to young adulthood and right up to the present. You will move from chores to jobs, like mowing lawns or babysitting, and starting to get paid for your work. After age 16 you may have had a job at a store in your community. As you graph your career, there will have been bosses, supervisors, and coworkers. You liked some and not others. Some treated you well, others didn't. All of that goes on your graph.

When the graph is done, you will convert the events and people into one or more of the three recovery categories and figure out the statements you will make in your Completion Letter. Here's an example of a comment you might need to make about a boss you had when you were a teenager: "For years I resented you for sending me home that day I was late. But I really learned from it. Ever since then I take my commitments seriously and always show up on time. I forgive you for sending me home; and I thank you for teaching me an invaluable life lesson."

It is not uncommon in today's corporate world to have been let go or downsized, even when you had been a good employee. Often, the communication about your termination was delivered without much apparent concern for you or your well-being or for your emotional reaction. With that in mind, forgiveness is often a huge element of completion.

When you're ready to write your Completion Letter you can use the open-ended format to start your letter: "I have been reviewing my relationship to my career and have found some things I want to say." As we showed in the faith section, your graph and letter will be about a series of relationships with many people, those who affected your work life. One of the common issues in career matters is that our hopes, dreams, and expectations of what would happen in our work life don't always come true. Use this Completion Letter to say "good-bye" to the old dreams, which will allow you to create new ones that are achievable.

As with other completions, we cannot stress enough how important it is to say "good-bye" at the end of this letter. One method is to issue a general comment that is aimed at everyone involved, which might look like this: "I have to go now, and I have to let go of any pain I have associated with my career, and with any of the people involved. Good-bye."

## Loss of Health—Health Changes

This section, like the last one, is based on the same ideas we showed in the loss of faith section at the beginning of this chapter. Please take the time to go back and read that section so you'll have an idea of the format that will also work on your health issues.

Once more, we're going to take you back to the beginning, your beginning. We want you to graph your relationship to your physical self. As a little boy or little girl, were you athletic? Were you a dancer? Did you do a lot of physical things? If the answer to any of those questions is yes, beginning your graph will be relatively easy. You will remember the things you liked doing. You will remember the people you did them with. Note: You may not remember all the names of people you played with as a child, and you may not remember exactly when you did certain things. That's okay. We're more concerned about the emotions of joy or pleasure—or pain—you had in using your body.

As you got a little older and began maturing, you may have had either a positive or negative sense of your body, how it looked, and what you thought others perceived about you. You also may have had many illnesses or conditions that restricted you from playing and otherwise using your body—even for hiking or biking or swimming. To the degree that you enjoyed doing physical things, there will have been a corresponding sense of loss when you couldn't do them.

For those of you who were not physical—who did not play sports, dance, or do many outdoor activities—your relationship graph about your body and health will be slightly different. There are many people whose great joys in life are more cerebral than physical. But even so, certain health problems may have limited your ability to read or use a computer or pursue whatever you loved doing. This is not to suggest that you had no relationship to your body or health, nor that diminishing health doesn't also affect you a great deal. In fact, it is sometimes the loss of certain physical abilities that makes some people aware that they had never made enough time for doing physical things.

In any case, as you graph your relationship to the physical things you did, there will usually be other people involved. In sports, there will have been teammates, coaches, and others who were part of that world. Again, you will have liked some of them, and not others. Each of them is part of a mini-relationship that you might need to address. "Thanks for being a supportive teammate. I remember your constant encouragement, it really helped me." Or, "You never helped me be part of the team. I forgive you for being so selfish."

For many people, sports, hiking, dancing, and other active pursuits are balancing events in their lives that help them reduce the pressures caused by work and other concerns. The use of our bodies can be very therapeutic to get us out of our heads. Losing the ability to be physically active can be a tremendous loss and should not be overlooked or minimized. It is also common that when our health diminishes, we lose a sense of independence that is part of being physically healthy. Don't overlook the fact that certain health conditions restrict our ability to drive a car, which also robs us of a sense of independence. Loss of health, more than most factors, causes people to feel vulnerable and with that comes a loss of safety.

When you write the Completion Letter, some of your emotionally important statements will be to the people who were part of the physical aspects of your life. But some of what you need to say will be more directed at your own body. Although it may seem silly, we think it a good idea to thank your body for all the pleasure you had using it to do the activities that pleased you. In the career section we mentioned that the Completion Letter was a good place to say "good-bye" to the hopes and dreams we once had that can no longer be, so we can develop new hopes for things we can achieve. The same is true with health issues. It's important to use this graph and letter as an opportunity to say good-bye to what we once were able to do, so we can focus on what we can do now.

In addressing the issues of your health, you might realize that some of what has occurred bears a relationship to whether or not you took good care of your body. If so, the graph and letter are the ideal places for apologizing to yourself for that lack of care. We know it can seem a little silly, but do it anyway. Some people prefer to forgive themselves, rather than apologize. It's your choice.

One last point: Many people acquire negative ideas about their bodies or about their athletic or physical abilities and skills from parents, siblings, or others. Those images can affect them throughout their lives, and limit what they do relative to the physical aspects of their lives. Again, the graph and letter are ideal places to forgive those people who set us up to limit ourselves in relationship to our bodies and our health and activities.

## MOVING

Moving may be the most overlooked of all grieving experiences. In order to understand why, you simply need to apply our definition of grief, which is *the conflicting feelings caused by a change or an end in a familiar pattern of behavior*. Nothing represents that definition more than moving, where everything familiar to you changes.

The best way to show you is to reprint a section from our book, *When Children Grieve,* which featured a first-person story about John W. James and his family. While it may seem to be focused on John's son, it is equally relevant to all, regardless of age.

*In 1987, John, his wife, Jess, and their six-year-old son, Cole, were preparing to move from an apartment in one area of Los Angeles to a house in a new neighborhood. By this time, John had been helping grieving people for many years, and he knew that grief can be defined as the conflicting feelings caused by a change or an end in a familiar pattern of behavior.*

*John had long since recognized that the first move from one home to another is one of the most powerful loss experiences affecting children. He knew that it did not matter if the new house or apartment was bigger and nicer than the old one. He also knew that it did not matter if the move was from one city or state to another, or simply from one part of town to another.*

*Children often struggle with change, for change can be scary. Moving automatically represents changes in everything that is fa-*

miliar to a child. Guess who is also affected? If you said the parents, you would be right.

Often when there is a move, it can mean that there is more money and the move is to a larger house. Those are positive things. However, regardless of its size or condition, children are accustomed to the old place. They know the home, and it seems to know them. They know every nook and cranny, for it is their home. The exciting feelings about the new home are mixed up with sadness about leaving the old one. Even if the children did not love the old home, they were very familiar with it. That mixture of positive and negative feelings illustrates what we mean by the phrase "conflicting feelings."

Sometimes fortunes are reversed, and the move is from a larger house to a smaller one. This move not only represents a change in the familiar but also adds the negative feelings associated with financial difficulties. Although young children may not recognize or relate to the money problems, they will be affected by their parents' attitudes. Children often hear parents' late night arguments about money. Or, they have an awareness of nonverbal communications between parents that indicate that something is not right.

**It is wise to remember that all major changes create emotional energy in children and adults.**

Cole was excited about having a house with a yard and his own swimming pool. He was also excited about having a larger room. At the same time, Cole was sad to be moving away from the friends he had made at his old school and in his neighborhood. John knew that the move they were about to make was a golden opportunity to teach Cole how to deal with the confusing feelings he was experiencing.

John took his family on an emotional tour of their apartment.

*They talked about the things they had shared in each room. Cole very quickly got into the spirit of the occasion. They talked about the happy and sad experiences they had shared in each room. They thanked each room for keeping them safe and protecting them from the hot or cold weather. They remembered important things like when Cole had lost his first tooth, and when he first learned to write his own name. And as they left each room, they said "thank you" and "good-bye" to it.*

*This exercise wasn't just for Cole's benefit. John and Jess were able to remember and talk about many of their memories, both good and bad. The process was very helpful to all three of them. On moving day, with tears in his eyes, Cole waved good-bye to the only home he had ever known. Cole adapted very well to the new home. Having completed his relationship with the old apartment, he was able to develop a new relationship with his new house. John and Jess still have fond memories about the old apartment in which Cole spent his early years, and they have built many more wonderful memories in their new home.*

*Soon, Cole will go away to college. While his room at home will still be his on holidays and vacations, he will take the same actions he did thirteen years ago, recognizing that many of his day-to-day activities will change as the result of his move. John and Jess will be with Cole, and together they will remember the events of the past thirteen years. Most of his life will now be lived at his college dorm, where he will develop new familiar patterns of behavior. And you have probably already figured out what Cole will need to do four years from now.*

*Do It—Even If It Seems Silly*—We strongly recommend that when you move, you take the actions described in John's story above even if you don't have children. The most important thing is to not do it alone. Recall that John and Jess and Cole did it together, each of them talking about their own memories of each room in the apartment. Even if you've lived there alone, make sure you have a friend with you to listen while you talk about your memories and then say "good-bye."

We've seen countless examples of the negative affect on adults and children who do not properly complete their relationships to something as important as their homes. This simple exercise can help ensure a smooth transition to your next home.

One of the by-products of those actions is that you may discover some still unfinished emotions attached to other people and relationships from your past. You can use the actions you've learned in this book to go back and complete your new discoveries.

**Even if this exercise seems silly to you, we cannot over-emphasize its importance. Do it anyway.**

## MISCELLANEOUS TIPS

### How Many Entries on Loss History and Relationship Graphs and Letters?

We are often asked how many entries there should be on a Loss History Graph or Relationship Graph. Since people are so different, there is no exact or correct answer. One difference relates to personal style. John tends to both speak and write with a limited amount of words. Russell tends to be more wordy. If you look at their respective Loss History and Relationship Graphs in this book, you'll see that difference. John has 9 entries on his Loss History while Russell has 13. John has 8 entries on his Relationship Graph with his brother, and Russell has 12 on his relationship with his former wife. Keep in mind those are all sample graphs to demonstrate the technique and don't represent the full length of the original graphs. But they do reflect the style difference between John and Russell.

There is no hard and fast rule for how many entries should be on any graph. The objective is accuracy not volume. We've known people who put too many entries on a Loss History or Relationship Graph and didn't get the benefits of the graphs. They became repetitive and listed each and every example of similar things. That is not to say you might not have experienced an inordinate amount of losses due to death. One key for you would be to list the deaths of people with whom you had involved relationships. Without being judgmental, we would suggest that the death of your second cousin, whom you'd only met twice in your life, might not need to be on your Loss History Graph.

As to number of entries: a general guideline for a Loss History Graph is to have somewhere between 6 and 20 entries. Of the thousands of them we've seen, the average is probably about 15. If you get too much beyond that number, you might need to see if you're repeating similar events or including people with whom you had limited relationships.

The Relationship Graph might have between 5 and 15 entries above the line, and the same amount below the line. Depending on whether the relationship was essentially positive or negative, your graph may be focused primarily on one side or the other. But if you start having a large amount on either side, look to see if you're repeating the same kind of events over and over. There is no need to repeat the same things. That creates the danger of keeping you stuck in the pain or in an unrealistically positive picture of that relationship.

The same guidelines hold true for the Completion Letter you create from your Relationship Graph.

## Compassion vs. Negation

A cliché has slipped into modern language that can create real difficulties in achieving emotional completion. The phrase is: "He did the best he could with what he had to work with." Typically it is said about someone with whom you did not have a good relationship. Even though it may be intellectually true, it is not emotionally helpful. We've known people who've added that comment near the end of their Completion Letters, and then call us some time later to tell us they don't feel complete. In the letter they write, "You did the best you could with what you had to work with." When they do that, they inadvertently override the forgiveness they had issued earlier in their letters. Without realizing it, they are excusing bad behavior. The intellectual fact is that whatever people do is their best, otherwise they'd do something else. A sadder part of that fact is some people's "best" nearly destroyed us.

In fairness, either of your parents or others who raised you may have been victims of horrible childhoods of their own—and of people and events later in life. They may have been subjected to alcoholism, mental illness, or just plain cruelty. For that, you may have some compassion for them. But it's likely that while they dragged the impact of those situations through their lives, they also inflicted you with the by-product of what was done to them. In spite of what they did to you, and if you have a sense of compassion for what happened to them, there is a more helpful way to say it. Rather than excusing it by saying it was the best they could do, and thereby negating the forgiveness you issued earlier in your Completion Letter, you can say: "Dad, I have compassion for you and the things that affected you." This should be near the very end of your letter and should always come after you have issued all the necessary forgiveness.

## No Questions—Only Statements

Another danger in Completion Letters is to ask questions. Obviously, a question asked in a letter to a person who has died cannot be answered. We've seen people ask things like: "Dad, why didn't you take better care of your health?" Asking an unanswerable question like that, even a rhetorical one, leaves you incomplete. Since the objective of Grief Recovery is emotional completion, you don't want to set yourself up to fail by asking questions that can't be answered.

While it is clear that people who have died can't answer your questions, it is never recommended that you ask questions in Completion Letters to living people. We remind you that your letters should never be communicated to the living people you are addressing. That's because your letter will have forgiveness in it, which must never be done directly. Therefore, given the fact that the living person will not be hearing your letter, you can't get answers to any questions. That is not to say that you can't ask questions of living people when you see them or talk to them—that's your choice. Just don't ask questions in Completion Letters.

## Use the PS Letter for Additional Completion

It's possible that you've already done Relationship Graphs and Completion Letters about your parents and others who affected your life, but you may still feel incomplete. If so, go back and do some additional work focused on those aspects of the relationship that contributed to your losses of trust, safety, normalcy, and childhood. You can do a mini-graph and then a PS Letter about those elements of a relationship in which you recall events or situations that caused you to feel unsafe or untrusting.

There are specific guidelines for PS Letters on pages 158–160, under the heading, *What About New Discoveries? Cole's Win-*

*dow Story*. John's PS Letter to his father demonstrates that you don't have to go back and redo the entire relationship graph and letter, you just have to deal with the particular situation that has come up.

After you write the mini-graph and PS Completion Letter, you must make sure to read your letter out loud to another living person, who qualifies as a "safe listener" for you. Use the Listening and Reading guidelines on pages 152–154.


## THE FINAL WORD

Recovery from grief or loss is achieved by a series of small and correct action choices made by the griever. We are heartened by having had this opportunity in the twentieth anniversary edition to pass along some additional guidance to help you take those actions.

We know that many people will read this book, enjoy it, and benefit from it. But they will not take the actions of recovery. We feel honored that you have read and appreciated this book. We would feel even better if you would go back and take the recovery actions, with or without a partner. Please don't allow the experience of reading and understanding to lull you into the idea that you are complete. Completion is the result of action.

As always, you have our support and our respect for your courage and willingness.

*John W. James*
and
*Russell Friedman*

# The Grief Recovery Institute: Services and Programs

The Grief Recovery Institute and thousands of affiliates offer a variety of programs for grievers. Certified grief recovery personnel facilitate Grief Recovery Outreach Programs in cities large and small throughout the United States and Canada. Programs are beginning in other parts of the world.

The Grief Recovery Outreach Program is designed to assist grievers in completing the pain caused by any major loss. The Outreach Program is ideal for anyone who has difficulty finding a partner to do the work outlined in this book.

Grief recovery certification authorizes the use of our registered trademark. Look for Grief♥Recovery®. It is your assurance that the facilitator has direct access to us and uses our program as designed.

The Grief Recovery Institute is the training facility for the certification program.

The Grief Recovery Institute conducts intensive seminars for grievers nationwide and provides speakers for a wide variety of organizations.

For information on any of our programs, please contact us.

In the United States:
Grief Recovery Institute
PO Box 56223
Sherman Oaks, CA 91403
(888) 773-2683

We also hope that you will visit us on the World Wide Web. Our home page is located at:

www.griefrecoverymethod.com

You may also E-mail us at: info@griefrecoverymethod.com

# *Acknowledgments*

**From John:**

After thirty years, there are far too many people to thank individually. But there are some from the past who cannot go unmentioned. I would personally like to acknowledge: Tommy Atkinson, Dan Brintlinger, John Borgwardt, Duane Chambers, and Steve and Terry Huston. They must receive special recognition and my personal thanks for the early days. I want to thank Frank Cherry, my first partner, who was there at the start.

This revised edition has its own list of people to thank. They are: Jonathan Diamond, our agent, and Trena Keating, our highly skilled yet fun-on-the-phone editor at HarperCollins.

I need and want to thank my partner and friend, Russell. He is the volunteer who wouldn't go away. Now he is my partner in our mission. We laugh and cry together and somehow manage to keep bringing our message of hope to those who need it the most.

I want to thank both my children. Allison was twelve the

last time I wrote an acknowledgment. During the last twenty years, I closed my eyes for what I thought was a short time. When I opened them again, she was beautiful, magnificent, and twenty-two years old. Twenty years ago, our son Cole was only six. Once an interviewer asked him if he knew what his daddy did. He thought for a moment and said, "My daddy helps sad people." He was right then, and he's still right. He's now twenty-six years old, 6'2", and 190 pounds. I cannot tell you how much I love them both.

I need and want to thank the tens of thousands of grievers who've shared their pain, hopes, and dreams with me. I am honored. Without their honest participation, there is no way the Grief Recovery Institute could have become so successful and reached so many hurting people.

How can I possibly acknowledge and thank my wife, Jess Walton? After my son died, I thought I would never get to experience joy again. Just like so many others, I laughed on the outside while crying on the inside. Then Jess came into my life. She has stood by me through all these years. She has joyfully supported this pioneering effort to help grievers. She's put up with my travel, long hours, and crying people in the living room. She even goes on game shows to win money for her favorite charity, the Grief Recovery Institute, when the phone bill is overdue and out of sight. During all this, she's continued to work in her chosen field of acting. She has won much acclaim from her fans and her peers. We even have two Emmy Awards on the mantel. She is a glamorous person in a glamorous profession, and there's nothing glamorous about what I do. I know she understands how much I love and appreciate her, but I want to thank her and tell her, I love you, anyway.

—*John W. James*